G000026213

#TBH

Basic Challenges
to Millennials
Who Can't Even

Regan Blanton King

abbott press

Abbott Press books may be ordered through booksellers or by contacting:

Abbott Press
1663 Liberty Drive
Bloomington, IN 47403
www.abbottpress.com
Phone: 1 (866) 697-5310

ISBN: 978-1-4582-2159-9 (sc)
ISBN: 978-1-4582-2158-2 (hc)
ISBN: 978-1-4582-2157-5 (e)

Library of Congress Control Number: 2018900939

Printed in the United States.

Abbott Press rev. date: 07/31/2018

Contents

Acknowledgements

Thank you to all at Abbott Press who have helped make the publishing process of this book as simple as possible. Thank you to all my family and friends who have faithfully prayed for me, persevered with me, and helped me in day to day life and in the writing of this book. Thank you particularly to my brother Ryan. Along with his many responsibilities as pastor of Grace Baptist Church in Wood Green and in working with Euro Evangelism he helped clean up some areas of this work. Thank you to The Angel Church for your patient, persevering, and prayerful support of me as a pastor in the church and in giving me the ability to study and address matters such as those discussed in this book. Thank you to my friends and colleagues at Christian Concern. Most of you are millennials and it is a privilege to work with others who defy generational norms and put Christ over culture. It would also be remiss of me to leave out my friends at Appestat coffee shop on Camden Passage in Angel, Islington and at Pret-A-Manger on 402 St. John Street. Your conversations and coffee kept me fueled as I undertook my writing.

For Dad and Mom - Barry and Frances King. You've never failed to challenge me when I'm wrong and to encourage me when I'm right. Thank you.

Introduction

Have you ever opened a book, skipped the table of contents, preface, and introduction, and gone straight to 'Chapter 1'? I used to do that too. Then I realised that to do so is to fail to properly read a book - particularly if the introduction is by the author and/or is a part of the original work.

The introduction sets the scene for what is to come. The introduction provides crucial information regarding the point and purpose of the book. The introduction is like an appetiser is to a fine meal. Sure, you can go right to the main course, but a suitable appetiser can complement and even enhance what is to follow.

Think of memorable movies - something like *Star Wars* or Christopher Nolan's *Dark Knight* trilogy. These always begin with a memorable introduction that can thrill, raise questions, and leave you wanting more. I remember going to see The Dark Knight with my Dad and twin brother. I was looking forward to it, but was slightly doubtful about how good the movie would be and was even more questioning about the quality of Heath Ledger's Joker. Within the first 5 minutes, I was gripped, thrilled, had tons of questions that needed answered, and was psyched for what I began to see would be one of my favourite movies and perhaps one of the best supporting actor roles in history (Ledger's Joker).

Would you pay for a three course set meal and skip the appetiser? Would you go to the cinema and intentionally miss the first 5 minutes of a movie? Then why skip a book's introduction? The introduction gives answers to initial and important questions - 'who?', 'what?', 'when?', 'where?', 'why?', and 'how?'. Through answering these questions perhaps you will have a better idea of where I'm coming from and will be better able to track along.

Who?

Allow me to take a little longer to introduce myself. If you looked at the author's name on the cover you will know that I am Regan Blanton King. I value my full name and on most occasions use my middle name as it reminds me of my Grandpa on my Dad's side whose middle name I share.

My first name is Irish and is said in the same way as the former American president (Reagan). My ancestry from the past few hundred years is part Irish and part Cherokee (Native American). I was born in 1992 in Little Rock, Arkansas and have lived in Hot Springs, Heber Springs, and Tumbling Shoals, Arkansas where I spent the primary formative years of my childhood. It was in this time my family was at Tumbling Shoals Baptist Church that I came to realise that God was real, I had sinned against him, but through Jesus Christ I could be reconciled to Him and saved from my sin, shame, and its consequences.

I moved to London, England in 2003 where my family became involved in inner city church planting. My father and mother are Christians and raised me and my siblings in a well-disciplined, well-ordered, loving environment where the virtues of undying and unconditional love, respect, honour, perseverance, integrity and honesty were instilled and held in the highest regard. I grew up with a love of sport, both team and individual. As a child I played Baseball, Basketball, and American football. As an adult, I still love keeping up with these and alongside regular gym exercise and periodic dabbling in Krav Maga, I am thrilled when I can play Basketball, football (international), cricket, and tennis (probably can't be called 'playing' - it's not my strong suit). I also like to challenge myself through participating in the occasional 5k, 10k and various obstacle races (eg. Tough Mudder). I am also in the process of teaching myself to play the electric guitar.

I have been involved in evangelism and outreach with numerous church planting projects, actively preaching since 2010 and acting in a pastoral role at The Angel Church in Angel, Islington, London since then as well. In 2014 this role became my full-time occupation and I became the pastor upon the church's constitution in 2016. I enjoy reading, writing, art (I paint and draw as a side hobby), and good cinema. My favourite superhero is Batman for reasons which I will not reveal lest I come across as too much of a nerd (ok, the general reason is that anyone can be Batman...if they have the time and money).

I am a normal guy. I have my issues. I am a sinner become a saint through Jesus Christ (read the New Testament letter *Ephesians*). My heart's desire is to live my life devoted to the cause of Christ and his glory through the growth of His kingdom on earth. Such a life is scarred and attacked by various problems and difficulties, not the least of which is regular rejection. Nevertheless it is a life ultimately free of regrets. It is a life that enjoys the good in the here and now, but looks forward the far better there and then of the new earth God will create (2 Peter 3.13).

What?

The goal of this book is not to excuse myself or others in my generation by way of some psycho-babble apologetic that puts blame for our issues and very real problems on previous generations or 'family dynamics'.

While highlighting some of the factors which have influenced certain beliefs and behaviours of millennials, my primary goal is to provide an answer and explanation for some issues faced particularly by millennials who profess to be Christians.

I desire to challenge the idea that to be 'free-thinking' is good and healthy and hope that this writing inspires more 'true-thinking', with an appreciation that truth is objective and concrete, transcending every earthly dimension and barrier. This book is by me - a millennial - for millennials and those who find themselves in regular contact with millennials. While acknowledging the feelings of millennials, this book is not about feelings. It is about facts and the facts don't always care about your feelings,[1] though being awakened to facts can hopefully positively impact and change your feelings.

When?

This book was the result of about 12 thoughts that came to my mind that counteract millennials' often made-up reality.

I was taking a brisk walk into central London from my pad in Angel, Islington and was considering some of the fairly basic issues that can send millennial snowflakes into a momentous melt-down. Some of these are issues I have dealt with personally in myself. All are issues I have personally dealt with to some extent in my relationships with millennials.

An important question, though. What on earth is a millennial?

Let me put your mind at ease. Millennials are not aliens, nor are they the product of a government conspiracy (though that would be

---

[1] Hat-tip to Ben Shapiro for his repeated use of this phrase.

a delicious prospect given some millennials penchant for conspiracy theories). Millennials are the generation defined as being born between the early 80s and the year 2000. Much of what I address in the following pages, however, has come to light in the transition or lack thereof from adolescence to adulthood in the average millennial. So the stuff I deal with here only became truly apparent from the early 2000s and consistently through to now as the last millennials become legal adults.

Where?

Hopefully the following chapters will be of some value to you wherever you are in the world. That said, my personal experience and the source material I use is particularly rooted in the West. Much of the world being influenced at some point and in various ways by the West, I am sure that similar challenges posed by Western millennials will be faced elsewhere as well.

Why?

I don't particularly relish writing this book. There are several other writing projects I started before I even felt this book needed to be penned. I am concerned that the point of this book and its contents may be misunderstood and so the goal completely missed. So let me clarify.

First - I do not feel as if I am ahead of the curve in addressing this matter.

In my teen years, a very positive and purpose-filled book was circulating in Christian circles by Alex and Brett Harris called *Do Hard Things: A Teenage Rebellion Against Low Expectations*. It came as a real encouragement and helped me know that as a young man I was not alone in desiring to fulfil William Carey's challenge to 'Expect great things from God; attempt great things for God'.

Fast-forward about 10 years and the challenge remains. The only thing is that many millennials, and more relevantly to my concern here, Christian millennials, didn't get the memo. Not only are hard things shied away from, when hard things naturally happen there is mental meltdown and a complete lack of strength exhibited. This is when in millennial speak, "we can't even."

'Can't even' what? Exactly.

Second, this book is not meant to be cynical. I do desire to be honest, however, in assessing some very serious misconceptions that are being perpetrated and perpetuated among Christian millennials. A part of the millennial problem is the reality that we have been coddled, catered to, and handled with kid gloves for too long. The amount of apologetic articles informing employers what millennial employees want from them (last I knew the employer is the one who hires and fires on their terms) says a lot.

This mollycoddling is increasingly reflected in popular culture where the traditional bad guys are now being portrayed in not so black and white revisionist remakes as not really bad, but simply 'misunderstood'. You got that right my friends, Maleficent of *Sleeping Beauty* fame wasn't really evil at all. You can understand this by looking at things from her perspective. While a Disney retelling doesn't really matter in and of itself, it is clear that popular culture reflects where society is currently at. That is increasingly troubling.

As a Christian who is also slotted in by society as a millennial, I hope that this book gees up other Christian millennials, challenging them to not be conformed by society's low expectations for our generation. Do not conform to culture's sociological psycho-babble terms and conditions that excuse our 'weaknesses' and wrongdoing.

Our world says 'love your weaknesses'. Jesus says 'repent' and 'follow me'. Jesus brings the needed change the world denies and decries. Do not allow yourself to be defined by your generational grouping and its unique attributes. Be defined by Christ and His Word. These are the foundational principles on which this book stands. This is the foundation on which I, a millennial, desires to be defined for God's glory and the good of myself and others until my dying day.

How?

In the following pages I seek to be real with 'free spirit' pseudo-Christian millennials. I wish to speak with honesty and in a way that will provide a punch where needed and a hand up if desired. There is a measure of responsibility on you, the reader's part. You need to search yourself and be as open-minded about my assessments as you claim to be about everything else under the sun. You need to pray and ask God to help you repent and right the areas in your life where you have misrepresented, mischaracterized, misattributed, and misapplied who He is and who He has called you to be if you are in Christ.

You and I have 'missed it' in many ways and that matters for us and even for the next generation. You may very well be reading this book and toss it away thinking it's not relevant to you and who you are. That may well be true. If so, pray for those of us for whom it is relevant and for whom it does matter significantly and seek out those areas where by God's grace you can change for the good. I aim to write in an easy going way that keeps things brief and to the point (millennials have a notorious short attention span) and prayerfully hope that this serves to encourage, inspire, correct, and stir you up to love and good works.

With love and friendship

Regan

Chapter 1

Yes, Christianity is religion

f you skipped the Introduction, go back and read it you thoughtless, lazy individual. Ok, perhaps that is a little OTT, but I didn't just write it for kicks or to fill out pages. It's there for a reason. Read it. (If you did skip, perhaps you can INSTAGRAM a pic of this page and transparently confess to your misdemeanour with the hashtags #skippedit #suitablyshamed….or not…just an idea.)

Yes, you read the chapter title correctly. Christianity is a religion and features religion. Totes devs.[2] How do you define religion? You and I don't earn special life perks that allow us to make up our own definitions for words as we go along.

---

[2] Whenever you come across a term such as this that you do not know, count yourself blessed and then look at the end of book glossary of Millennial terms. I am sorry this exists.

Just Google 'religion definition'. The top three definitions given are:

1. The belief in and worship of a superhuman controlling power, especially a personal God or gods.
2. A particular system of faith and worship
3. A pursuit or interest followed with great devotion

Christianity is the belief in and worship of the God of the Bible and all that entails. It is monotheistic. There is one Triune God. He[3] is personal and relational. He is all powerful and is in control. Christianity is a particular system of faith and worship with its foundation in the Old Testament and God's special relationship with the descendants of Abraham, Isaac, and Jacob (Israel). This foundation is filled up and completed in the New Testament with Jesus Christ fulfilling God's promises to Abraham, Isaac, Jacob, Moses, and David in particular.

The whole of the Old Testament points to God's promises and the nature of their fulfillment in the coming Messiah or Christ. The whole of the New Testament is the testimony of how we can know that the Messiah is Jesus who was born of the virgin Mary, lived sinlessly, died on the cross taking our sin on himself, and is resurrected assuring us of God's grace and mercy to all who repent of sin and place faith in Him.

Alongside this testimony is the crystal clear example of how the early church operated and worshipped. Read the New Testament book commonly called *Acts*. Read church history books that value primary

---

[3] No apologies if this triggered anyone who questions why God is referred to in the masculine. It is who God is and how He self identifies. Why shouldn't we respect how God identifies Himself?

sources.[4] These clearly show the gathering of Christians together as a church in particular local places.

Yes, they did meet together. Yes, worshipping on 'the Lord's Day' - mattered and was the norm. Yes, they engaged in practices that some may refer to as rituals, though they were practiced in meaning-filled ways with Christ as the centre of worship. Yes, baptism as believers mattered - indeed it is the only baptism of which the Scriptures speak. Yes, there were those recognised as members of the church body and those who were not. Yes, songs were sung, Scriptures read, and prayers prayed. Like it or not, sermons were preached and some went on for a pretty long time. Yes, fellowship meals were held and the elements of the Lord's Table observed by those who were baptised believers in good standing with the local church.

The Apostle Paul cautioned against making the Lord's Table a full, albeit special, meal - something many millennials I have met seem to entertain returning to without thinking through why it was abandoned. People were abusing the time and were gorging themselves and getting drunk while others had nothing. The goal of the Lord's Table was not to eat and drink to fullness or past fullness, rather it was an act of remembrance. Hence the reason, whether preceded by a fellowship meal or not, most churches to this day partake in token symbols of the body and blood of Jesus in the form of an unleavened bread cube and a small cup of grape juice or wine.

All of this originates in the New Testament and all of it fits the Googled definition 'religion'.

---

[4] Nick Needham's *2000 Years of Christ's Power,* Volume 1 (Grace Publications, 2004) is one such excellent source that relies heavily on sources dated in the first centuries AD.

Christianity is the pursuit of holiness in Christ by God's grace through faith. It is an all-consuming interest. Real devotion sees great sacrifice. Real devotees are so convinced of the value in their pursuit they rarely will consider their sacrifices as loss - such is the value of life, hope, and help in Christ and his promises.

Devotion goes beyond commitment, it spends itself sacrificially for the cause it is sold out to. In Christianity the spirit of this devotion can be summed up with the words 'for me to live is Christ and to die is gain' (Philippians 1.21). If we live, we will seek to live for Christ's fame and glory. If we die in the process, our death is only gain. In Christ, death loses its sting so what is there to fear? (1 Corinthians 15:55)

'But the Bible never speaks of following Christ as religion. It is all about relationship!' runs the objection of the average contrarian, debate-hungry millennial.

Really? Show me that in the Bible. You won't be able to make a convincing case unless you twist definitions to suit your preferred definition of 'religion'.

Certainly, Christianity is all about being reconciled in our relationship to God through Christ. We have been estranged from God our Father. We have run away. We have thrown away God's gifts and lived supremely for self. Jesus comes to make us right with God. Jesus calls us to turn around from the destruction, sin, and shame that characterises so much of our lives and enables us to run back to our Heavenly Father with whom we can enjoy a personal and fulfilling relationship.

As Christians who are a part of the bride of Christ, the church, we often wander away. As churches we often go off track and get things wrong. We can become estranged from our husband, Christ. We start doing things our way. We slide on our backs first to discouragement, then to despondency, then to disillusionment, and very often then to destruction evidenced in departing from the faith.

The Holy Spirit, keeps those of us who are truly born again safe from the final destructive element, and mercifully we can be reconciled to Christ again, knowing he is good, gracious, and will not give up on His people.

As Hosea (Old Testament prophet) was faithful to his whore-wife Gomer and welcomed her back in love, so Jesus' faithfulness remains and he welcomes us back in love. As the Prodigal son's father ran to meet his repentant son with rejoicing, there is rejoicing in heaven when one of God's wayward children returns (Luke 15:11-32).

So yes. The Bible talks a lot about our relationship with God and has different pictures for illustrating this (Father/estranged son and Husband/unfaithful wife). What's more it makes it very clear that being right in our relationship with God enables us to be right in our relationships with each other. It sets a model for reconciliation, renewal, and righteousness in any sphere of relating to our fellow man whether in the home, the workplace, or just chilling with your bros.

To agree that Christianity is all about relationships is not to deny that it is very much a religion, particularly when the Bible *does* speak of Christianity as a religion and defines what real and pure religion should look like. James writes:

> If anyone thinks he is **religious** and does not bridle his
> tongue but deceives his heart, this person's **religion** is

> worthless. **Religion** that is pure and undefiled before
> God the Father is this: to visit orphans and widows in
> their affliction, and to keep oneself unstained from the
> world. (James 1:26-27)

James acknowledges that some people's religion is worthless, invalid, and hypocritical. Nevertheless he does not throw the baby out with the bath water. James affirms that there *is* pure religion that is right and undefiled and that is desired and good before God.

The evidence James gives of pure religion should not be extracted from its historical and cultural context and misapplied. Millennials could look at this and conclude Christianity is all about social justice. Let's start some protests and stuff and let's change the world. Let's have a 'die-in' somewhere and show we care. Without denying the importance of justice in society or appropriate democratic campaigning action, this isn't at all what James is talking about.

Widows and orphans were on the scrap heap of society. Literally. Seriously. They would often sit outside the city gates on refuse heaps begging. They were hated and considered worthless. They were discounted by anyone and everyone as Grade A, 1ˢᵗ class losers with a capital 'L'. James' call is to a revolution in attitude towards these people. He calls for them to be cared for and loved with the compassion of Christ. This would have been explicitly Christ-centric as opposed to self-congratulating moral kindness.

Often overlooked in this is James' call to 'keep oneself unstained from the world.' Certainly, this is linked to James' previous call to be doers as well as hearers of God's word and relates to his statement 'Faith without works is dead' (James 22:14-26). Similarly, it cannot be separated from the context of the Christian church community from which and to which James is so clearly writing.

Throughout the New Testament any idea of 'lone-ranger' Christianity is shunned. 33 individual local churches are mentioned by name in the New Testament along with 6 regions where there were clusters of local churches (eg. Galatia). Hebrews 10:25 is a pointed and specific call to not be like those who avoid gathering for worship in church. Indeed, the principle of church and its gathering is a consistent remedy to the reality that 'the one who isolates himself breaks out against all sound judgement.' (Proverbs 18:1)

Yes Christianity is all about relationship and those relationships are all defined by 'religion that is pure and undefiled.' Get over it and get out there and live it unashamedly.

Chapter 2

Yes, rules do matter

Millennials have a complicated relationship with rules.

On one hand, it's totes obvs that rules matter. You wouldn't just show up at your Ultimate Frisbee tournament grudge match and not follow the rules would you? You would certainly find it hard to play your *Monopoly: The Legends of Zelda Collector's Edition* or *Settlers of Catan* properly without rules. It's up to you whether you formally keep score and declare a winner at the end of the game or not, but in your heart you know that in following the rules there are literal winners and losers.

That said, millennials often act like everyone should get a medal for living life, whether by the rules or not! On another level, millennials are ok with rules...so long as they make them. In yet another millennial subculture, rules are to be challenged and in many cases hated. Breaking rules frees yourself from the status quo and the slavery of social expectations.

Let's acquaint ourselves with these different types of millennials.

Adulting millennials

What about the so-called 'game of life'? I mean, rules are, like, a core part of adulting right?

Adulting?

Wait. You *do* know what I'm talking about?

Just in case you are a millennial who has been fortunate enough to not come across this term, I apologise now for introducing it to you. I deny any liability that may result from your exposure to this freakishly zombified social construct. Please don't faceplant too hard at the definition.

Slang-savvy and web-based *Urban Dictionary* defines 'adulting' as "to do grown up things and hold responsibilities such as, a 9-5 job, a mortgage/rent, a car payment, or anything else that makes one think of grown ups."

Perhaps you are blown away by this definition. Maybe you are even a little confused. If so, you probably understood the definition. To clear any confusion up, let's use it in a short mock social media post by someone we will refer to as 'Millennial Mike' who is 28.

> 'Wow! Rad day today bros. Got up early - like 8.00am lol! Made it to work on time rofl and stayed 15 minutes over. Got home, paid some bills, fixed a meal, swept the floor, washed my undies, and ironed some clothes all before chilling to netflix. Got this adulting thing nailed. #adulting.'

Yes. You read that right. Millennial Mike had a pretty standard day doing normal things that any able bodied teenager should know how to do let alone an adult. What is also more than a little disturbing is that Millennial Mike has also felt a self-congratulatory public pat on the back in the form of a Facebook post is in order.

Well done Mike. Well done for doing something that is literally standard adult behaviour. You clearly know the rules of being an adult...but most adults don't act like doing laundry is a rule of life that when fulfilled deserves a mention much less a medal.

My way or the highway millennials

Of course rules matter. So long as you make the rules. A 2012 TIME magazine article notes several characteristics of the average millennial in working environments.[5]

1. Millennials require your immediate attention.
2. Millennials want casual Fridays almost every day.
3. Millennials work when they want to work.
4. Millennials aren't all about the money.
5. Millennials really like transparency.
6. Millennials see the work environment as flat.

In the first instance, instant-access news, and the ever-plugged in and present nature of life on Facebook, Twitter, and Instagram has produced an unhelpful, time-consuming, me-centric attitude to the workplace. Previously, workplaces functioned with a manager who gave instructions that were fulfilled. In an office full of millennials, the manager must also play role of mentor and with particularly needy

---

[5] Dan Schawbel, 'Millennials vs. Baby Boomers: Who Would You Rather Hire?' in Time (29 March, 2012)

individuals, mother. If this expectation is not fulfilled, millennials can become unsatisfied and leave.

The second shows a lack of social awareness. Go on and moan about limiting social constructs, but there are appropriate forms of work attire for different jobs. If you are working in a job that requires a tie but you want to wear a t-shirt you have one of two options a) grow up and wear the tie as the management requests, no questions asked or b) find a job that allows you to wear a t-shirt.

This same trend of overt casualness has crept like a cancer into almost every sphere. Sure, I love wearing my hoodies, t-shirts, and jeans. I am a fairly laid back and casual guy. But when I am working in the city, meeting a former boss or colleague for a nice meal, or attending a wedding celebration I do have an understanding of what is expected and appropriate and I will not draw unnecessary attention to myself by rocking up in my everyday clothes.

As for work - I understand the philosophy behind flexible working hours and do quite like the idea. That said, here are the facts. If you accept a job that is described as 9-5, you need to work 9-5. It's called respect. It shows a realisation that the business is not your own. If you want a different schedule or are discontent with your office's rules, start your own business. Of course you will not be the first millennial to do just that. The referenced TIME article asserts: "Half of the members of Gen Y surveyed said they would "rather have no job than a job they hate." This may help explain why unemployment of millennials is 40% higher in the US than Generation X.[6]

---

[6] Life lesson: You can't always start with the job you love. From personal conversations with fellow millennials I think quite a few missed the memo.

Finally, transparency - while important in business - has its bounds. It is not the human right of a receptionist, errand girl, or janitor, to know why the CEO or manager has made a particular decision. And yet millennials seem to crave being at the centre of a company's vision as they, after all, are more in touch with the world today. This attitude has led me to conclude that millennials, also known as 'Generation Y' could accurately be dubbed 'Generation Why' or 'Generation Whine".

Perceived lack of transparency and the incessant complaining of millennials in the workplace could also add to the toxic atmosphere that makes a workplace feel flat, likely contributing to high staff turnover.

Rule-breaking millennials

Rule-breakers are awesome. Anarchy rocks! I mean, it's like really cool when someone just doesn't give a care what others may think or feel about them or their behaviour. So rad. If someone looks at you and sees something that goes against their ridiculous expectations, that person's the one with the problem not you. Don't even give them the time of day - you don't need that kind of negativity in your life.

Millennial singer Charli XCX sums it up nicely in her song *Break the Rules*:

I don't wanna go to school
I just wanna break the rules
Boys and girls across the world
Putting on our dancing shoes
Going to the discotheque
Getting high and getting wrecked
I don't wanna go to school
I just wanna break the rules

Neato!

Scuffle….gasp..wallop...bang...shouts….groans...scuffle...smash...
unintelligible new-agey psycho-babble...shriek....door slam.

Apologies. Regan here again. I had to rescue this segment from someone who thought inserting his own thoughts into *my* writing was acceptable in today's 'free' society.

The reality is that rules are hated by your average millennial. They are seen as irrelevant, restrictive, and without point. Really, they are there to be broken.

Hear me out here. I am not talking about challenging faulty science and exploring beyond theoretical formulas. Certainly, much of modern technology has resulted from people pushing the boundaries of their current day's understanding of what was and was not possible. In previous times the very idea of an aeroplane would have been ridiculed and some would have perhaps thought of it as sorcery as opposed to complex engineering. I say this because the natural reaction to this segment could be to come up with all the good things that have come of 'rule-breaking'. Chuck that instinct away and understand that these are not the sort of rules we are talking about.

We are talking about deliberately going against the grain of what is right and wrong with a flawed understanding that morality is relative or that right and wrong boils down to 'what you feel'. If you are reading this as someone who does not believe in God, much less the Christian God, this attitude is normal. It's an attitude that's existence is acknowledged in the New Testament passage Romans 1:18-23:

For the wrath of God is revealed from heaven against all ungodliness and unrighteousness of men, who by their unrighteousness suppress the truth. For what can be known about God is plain to them, because God has shown it to them. For his invisible attributes, namely, his eternal power and divine nature, have been clearly perceived, ever since the creation of the world, in the things that have been made. So they are without excuse. For although they knew God, they did not honor him as God or give thanks to him, but they became futile in their thinking, and their foolish hearts were darkened. Claiming to be wise, they became fools, and exchanged the glory of the immortal God for images resembling mortal man and birds and animals and creeping things.

The rules of right and wrong, true and false are known, but throughout history, mankind has tried to make his own way and it has seldom led anywhere good and in all cases has led away from the truth of God in Jesus Christ.

Scrap your neo-Christian millennial theology....please!

As a Christian considered by birth date to be a millennial I write this chapter prayerfully and primarily as a challenge to other Christian millennials who have embraced certain millennial trends including this idea that rules don't matter.

Rules do matter. Rules set a standard. Rules remind us of a right and a wrong way. Rules when observed can be difficult, but when you follow them you understand they are so much more than just rules.

So why should you value rules?

The Bible is full of rules.

Can you name the 10 commandments? Try listing them right now. Keep an accurate count.

Paraphrased from Exodus 20 they are:

I am the Lord your God. You shall have no other gods before me.
You shall not make for yourself any idol to bow down to worship it.
You shall not take the name of the Lord your God in vain.
Remember the Sabbath Day and keep it holy.
Honour your father and mother.
Do not murder.
Do not commit adultery
Do not steal.
Do not bear false witness against your neighbour.
Do not covet.

Are these relevant for today? If you are struggling to answer just make it personal.

What if someone murdered your husband or other loved one? What if you found your spouse had cheated on you and watched as she walked hand in hand with her new boy, kissing and flirting away?

Bizarrely, many may try to avoid the question and refer to Jesus' words in Mark 12 in which he responds to a query as to what commandment is most important.

"What really matters is that we 'love God with all our heart, mind, soul and strength and love our neighbour as ourself.'"

Agreed. But did you notice what Jesus does there? He summarises the 10 commandments into 2. The 2 commandments that Jesus gives are fleshed out by the 10 commandments and the 10 commandments themselves are fleshed out by other specifics pertaining to morality. For example, adultery in the specific sense is not the only sexual sin in existence, but it serves as a good umbrella term for every sexual act that takes place outside of the lifetime marriage of a man and woman as husband and wife. One cannot go through the Old Testament without gaining the distinct impression that, yes, rules do matter and there is wisdom in heeding them (Proverbs drives this point home time and again.)

"But all of that is Old Testament. We are free in Christ. There are no more rules."

This may be your attitude and response right now. Before you throw shade, please show the open-mindedness that Millennials claim to have and consider that this just is not what the Bible teaches.

In the first place Jesus did not have a 'no more rules' philosophy. In his famed 'Sermon on the Mount' Jesus says

> Do not think that I have come to abolish the Law or the Prophets; I have not come to abolish them but to fulfill them. For truly, I say to you, until heaven and earth pass away, not an iota, not a dot, will pass from the Law until all is accomplished. Therefore whoever relaxes one of the least of these commandments and

teaches others to do the same will be called least in the kingdom of heaven, but whoever does them and teaches them will be called great in the kingdom of heaven. For I tell you, unless your righteousness exceeds that of the scribes and Pharisees, you will never enter the kingdom of heaven. (Matthew 5:17-20)

'But when Jesus said this, he hadn't yet fulfilled the law and prophets in his death, burial, and resurrection. After that we are free.'

Of course we are free. Paul says to the Galatian churches,

'For freedom Christ has set us free; stand firm therefore, and do not submit again to a yoke of slavery.' (Galatians 5:1)

What slavery? Paul indicates that the Galatians have strayed from obeying the truth (Galatians 5:7) which indicates that there is a rule that defines truth. It is concrete and immovable. He then says:

But I say, walk by the Spirit, and you will not gratify the desires of the flesh. For the desires of the flesh are against the Spirit, and the desires of the Spirit are against the flesh, for these are opposed to each other, to keep you from doing the things you want to do. But if you are led by the Spirit, you are not under the law. Now the works of the flesh are evident: sexual immorality, impurity, sensuality, idolatry, sorcery, enmity, strife, jealousy, fits of anger, rivalries, dissensions, divisions, envy, drunkenness, orgies, and things like these. I warn you, as I warned you before, that those who do such things will not inherit the kingdom of God. But the fruit of the Spirit is love, joy, peace, patience, kindness, goodness, faithfulness, gentleness, self-control; against such things there is no law. And those who belong to Christ Jesus have crucified the flesh with its passions and desires. (Galatians 5:16-24)

What Paul is saying is that there are certain rules that will be a reasonably righteous indicator as to whether you are right with God or not. Do not misunderstand. Following the rules of the Bible does not make you right with God. You and I have failed and sinned against God and His rules and it is only God's grace through faith in Christ that can save us. In that salvation, however, we are changed and transformed in our hearts and minds to where we value God's way and rules as good, right and true and will seek to live according to this. Indeed, the rules and our failure to keep them initially often lead us to Christ (Galatians 3:24). This means also that we will respect other people's conscience on areas not critical in the Christian life and will not ridicule or cast judgement (Colossians 2 and Romans 14). This means that we will respect authority even when we do not necessarily agree with it on everything (Romans 13).

Yes. Rules matter. Rules are a part of the healthy functioning of society and are a core part of constructively disciplining oneself. If you haven't been bothered with them before, perhaps it's the right time to seriously consider getting bothered with them now.

Chapter 3

Yes, structure is important

When it comes to structure for the average millennial, the struggle is real. Society just has way, way, way too much structure. Companies are still run by a bunch of dudes in suits. The ongoing presence of traditional family units featuring a husband, wife, and a child or children is an irksome reminder of the biological clock as well as the source of some conviction at one's own lack of stability. But that's all part of being 'progressive'.

A random and very scattered rant by Millennial Mike could look something like this:

> "Stepping outside the 'gender binary' and promoting fluidity creates all manner of relationship options, but it will take time. People still want to maintain punctual timekeeping, scheduling, and appointment making and get upset when kept waiting.

So ridiculous right? Everything seems so hierarchical. You have the CEOs, presidents, trustees, managers, assistant managers, and then basic employees. And they all get different pay. The CEO gets, like, 150k but the cleaner gets only 17k. What's with that? The whole structured time thing at work is crazy too. You just get up at the same time every morning, you go to work, you come home, you eat, you sleep, you have a little bit of time with family and/or friends...it's just so basic. It is not very colourful."

My millennial woes. Life isn't a rom-com. It often isn't very colourful. Sometimes you may think that the basic stuff of life is boring and mundane. There are seasons in life when not much seems to change and you just can't get turnt about much of anything. Why do you feel this way? What do you need to do to get it sorted?

Consider advice from Millennial Mandy (Mike's cousin) posted under an Instagram quote picture she posted after a google search for 'inspiring self-esteem quotes':

Scrap structure! Get rid of the ball-and-chain relationships which have structured your life too much and have helped you become a more disciplined, less fun you. Quit your job and just be yourself! You don't need the kind of negativity in your life that tells you how to work. Stop the gender binary. You will be surprised at how many more relationships you can have...sure most are pretty brief, but you will have an awesome time and stick two fingers up to those traditional family unit snobs. Don't worry about money or saving or that mess. You can't take it with you!

Just do with it what you want! Have a blast! Don't worry about sleeping in late. Remember, sleeping in late means brunch! I'm sayin. And why not make it a boozy brunch while you're at it? #LIFEHACK #SQUADGOALS

Hold on….that's basically right back where we started. We've not progressed at all in fact. The very things you may think dispatch structure ironically become their own structure. In trying to avoid 'becoming a statistic' you become a statistic with an ever-growing subculture of disconsolate individuals who flit insatiably to and fro from one thing to the next whether it be in work, family life, beliefs, or behaviour to satisfy their own fickle whims.

Previous generations would see such behaviour as socio or psychopathic in some degree. Some may see it as the result of a 'mid-life' crisis and the realisation of one's own mortality and the brief nature of healthy life. I'm not convinced millennials will know much about mid-life crisis though; the average millennial life seems to be one of permanent and primarily self-imposed crises of trying to find meaning, purpose, and community outside of structure.

Structureless life

No. 'Doing life' does not excuse laziness. Despite millennial protestations against the charge of laziness, 'stats don't lie.'[7]

Unemployment of millennials is 40% higher in the US than Generation X.[8] This could be explained by a few factors. 1) The idea that the

---

[7] Shout out to my brother, friend, and fellow church planter, Sonny Simak of Grace Church Southall for regularly reminding me of this.

[8] Eileen Patten, Richard Fry, 'How Millennials today compare with their grandparents 50 years ago' for Pew Research Centre (19 March, 2015)

employee is in the driving seat of a business rather than the employer 2) The dissatisfaction with traditional jobs leading to attempts to begin a 'start-up' and 3) Sheer laziness.

In relation to the first, I actually came across an article entitled 'A Millennial's Take on What Millennials Want From Employers.'[9] And here I thought employers were the ones who had the right to give the t's and c's! This relates very much to the previous chapter and the very real importance of rules. Read it again if necessary.

The second factor that leads to 'start-ups' is not nearly as negative, though there can be a tendency to 'start-up' upstart snobbery. Millennials *are* creating businesses at twice the rate of Boomers and Gen Xers (the success or failure of these is irrelevant here). Content editor for *Venngage* Ryan Mccreedy explains:

> Making our own work is the best way to take control of our situation...There were many things that I could not have learned at a traditional company. But I still felt shunned by some of the older people or colleagues just from taking an unconventional path. Even though I was working harder than most of them.[10]

Granted there is some validity to Mccreedy's observation:

> 89% of millennial workers are checking and responding to work emails outside of normal working hours. Additionally, 73% of millennials are expected to be

---

[9] Samara Parker, 'A Millennials Take On What Millennials Want From Employers' on *JobCast.net* (6 October, 2013)
[10] Ryan McCreedy, 'Millennials don't suck, you're just old and hate change' on *TheNextWeb.com* (7 June, 2016)

able to respond to calls or emails at any time. Unless I am sleeping, I always have my phone on my body or within reach. Gone are the days when you leaving the office meant work was over.

Attitude and motivation are important issues to consider here, but each millennial is responsible for these important factors as an individual. Enterprise and innovation are to be applauded, but both will fail if outweighed by ego and arrogance.

Crazy lazy

As for my third explanation for the high millennial unemployment rate, sheer laziness, in some ways this is harder to prove statistically. Regular interaction with unemployed millennials, I have found, is insightful. Some jobs are beneath millennials, so they just won't work...or almost worse still, they give up and quit.

A conversation with Millennial Mike could look something like the following:

'Hey bro! How are you?'
'Man, I just can't find a job. Not doing much at the moment. Just chillin.'
'About that, I know it may not be what you're looking for long term, but McDonalds is hiring.'
'Hahahaha. Serious bro?! Man you've got bare bantz'
back-slap
'Seriously. Its honorable work. Gives you something to do'
Wheezing and snorting with laughter
'Man, you wouldn't catch me dead with that job.'

'What? There is nothing wrong with it at all. Whatever though. Hey, have you considered volunteering? I know a few of the charity shops need some help and there are several community groups that could do with some aid...'

'Nah, that's not really the thing for me. I actually like to get paid for my work. You know what I mean? I like to be valued for the services I provide. Nah, that's not my ride brohim.'

'But it gives you something to do Mike. Keeps you busy. Keeps you from being lazy and idle'

'Trust me man, I swear-down I'm not lazy. Besides, Netflix keeps me busy, you know what I mean?'

Some figures do indeed imply laziness is at the very least a potential problem. The stats on television viewing among millennials are troubling.

According to Nielsen's Total Audience Report, millennials watch around 4 hours of television every day.[11] Statistics show that 35% of 14 to 25 year-olds binge-watch at least once a week, compared to the 25 percent of 33 to 49 year olds who report doing so. In many cases this means watching up to 6 episodes of an hour long television program, though it is not uncommon for millennials to try and kill a whole season in a single sitting or over a weekend. Done regularly, this paints a pretty sad picture of wasted time and a willingness to benefit from others' creativity rather than explore one's own in hobbies, art, or other forms of personal development.[12]

What's more, regular binge-watching is linked to increased feeling of depression and anxiety and millennials show higher rates of depression

[11] Nielson, 'The Total Audience Report: Q4 2015', (24 March 2016)
[12] Statista, 'Binge watching in the US', statista.com

than others.[13] 35% report lack of self-motivation as a barrier to physical exercise and 50% say they are too busy to work out [14] (the reported 18 hours a day average millennials spend on consuming media eats into time![15]) The dream gym of the future for millennials apparently 'is seen as a relaxed, interactive, customized and fun environment.'[16] Basically a place to 'free-style' not work-out. There is more to be discussed, but hopefully this begins to help you see that without suitable discipline and structure in life, you will suffer.

Structureless community

Yes, your version of community often looks like isolation. It's not fetch. It's not fetch at all.

Isolation through self

In trying to 'keep it 100' you often show that you are primarily absorbed with yourself. Maybe being true to yourself is finding yourself at the centre of other people's lives.

You are loud. You love a good put down of someone else. You question everyone and everything and have to have the last say about anything. You basically find it hard to just sit down and shut up even when appropriate and advisable. In those moments you are clueless as to the angst, frustration, confusion, hurt, or bewilderment you may be causing.

---

[13] Laura Heck, 'A generation on edge: A look at millennials and mental health' in *Vox Magazine*, 19 November 2015
Samantha Olson, 'Binge Watching TV Linked To Higher Rates Of Depression And Anxiety' in *Medical Daily*, 8 November 2015
[14] Technogym, 'The Wellness Deficit: Millennials and Health in America' 2015
[15] Kate Taylor, 'Millennials Spend 18 Hours a Day Consuming Media -- And It's Mostly Content Created By Peers' in *Entrepreneur*, 10 March 2014
[16] Technogym, The Wellness Deficit: Millennials and Health in America, 2015

In one way, you think structure in community is fine...so long as you provide the foundation on which the structure stands or falls. Your pride, arrogance, and aloofness to others' needs, feelings, and the reality that you are not the centre of gravity eventually isolates you. You realise you don't really have any meaningful friends and those friends you do have eventually leave you or you burn your bridges leaving them behind. You become alone, but you continue to plunge with passionate, headstrong, reckless abandon into the pursuit of your own happiness without considering others.

Isolation of self

Perhaps you are not the above 'type' of millennial. You are not the life and soul of the party. To be honest, you don't really 'do' parties. If you find yourself at a party, you look out of place, you feel uncomfortable, you don't make much effort to get to know others and you leave as soon as possible.

If you are at a wedding reception and everyone is dancing and having a good time, you are the person who sits on her own at a table and says 'I don't do that sort of thing. I hate loudness and it's just not fun. I'd rather just sit here.' If you are on holiday with family and there is time to spend with them, you'd prefer to just sit and remain plugged in to your phone or find somewhere to hide and read a book.

Maybe you are a blend of both of the above types. I can certainly relate to varying feelings of extroversion and introversion at different times on different days. I refuse to be defined by one or the other. I try to operate under the principle that there is a time and place for both and knowing that time and properly implementing it calls for much self-control, motivation, and discipline. I fail sometimes, probably more often than I care to admit, but hopefully am figuring it out more and more.

Why is discussion of these types important and why should millennials care? They are part of building structured, well-ordered communities made up of different personality types and functioning on respect and healthy face-to-face communication - communication that is all too lacking among Millennials. Consider the reality that

> "Communication is the source of all human growth and the key to human relatedness...The words 'communicate' and 'community', although verb and noun come from the same root. The principles of good communication are also the basic principles of community building".[17]

Communication probs.

"Seriously, are you saying that in this day and time when we have never been more connected we lack good communication and community?"

Well sussed Captain Obvious. That is exactly what I'm saying. Connected communication is no substitute for intimate community.

Think of two primary modern hubs for communities. The coffee shop and the pub.

Go to your local Starbucks. You will mostly see people plugged in and not talking at all with one another. Try to attempt a conversation with someone. Depending on where you are, you may be taken for a creep, mistaken for trying to hit on someone, or just a bit of a weirdo. People

---

[17] George Manning et al., *Building Community: The Human Side of Work*, (Duluth, Minnesota: Whole Person Associates, 1996) p 130

will talk with and to anyone and everyone apart from those next to them and there is little that can be done to reverse this trend.

Now go to a pub. It may be loud and depending on the time a bit raucous. People are laughing and chatting away and it seems like it may be the community you have been looking for. But think about it. In most cases the conversation and laughter has been facilitated by varying levels of intoxication.

On more than one occasion people have opened up and been honest with me about their life when intoxicated in such a way they would not have apart from the booze. One millennial actually voluntarily acknowledged this to me. "It feels like I'm only honest to you when I've had a few drinks" he told me after showing up at my house at 6.30 on a Saturday morning, having telephoned around 5.00am that same morning.

Communication built on intoxication does not provide healthy friendships or meaningful community. It does not aid the healthy functioning of well-ordered society because it is intrinsically dis-orderly.

It is no surprise that our versions of 'community' often lead us to feel more isolated. Our approach is haphazard and without structure. Structure in community matters. The Bible informs us of the community we really need and how it is to be structured. It is called the church, but we try our best to muck that up as well.

Structureless church

I love my church. It is a family of people who have dedicated themselves to one another's lives and to growing together in the knowledge and love of Jesus Christ. We sing together, pray, listen to Bible teaching, ask questions, discuss the Bible, encourage one another with Bible passages in the week, enjoy fun times out and about, eat together, play table-tennis, bananagrams, and football. We go through good and bad times together. We share burdens. We grieve together. We celebrate together. We carry one another.

Though still a small inner-city church in what has been dubbed 'post-Christian' England, we function with a healthy structure of recognised eldership, diaconate, and membership. We gather on Sunday morning at 10.00 am for prayer and Bible reading, then at 11(ish) we worship together as a congregation. On Tuesday we meet at 7.00 when we enjoy fellowship over quality coffee and snacks before opening God's Word together and discussing it in our quest to know more of who God is and who He desires us to be. While meetings are friendly and free-flowing, there is an order and organisation to them. There is leadership.

So old fashioned, right? Errm, try Biblically faithful. Increasingly, there is an idea that church shouldn't be structured. Some would say at all. This ecclesiological philosophy often, by definition, abandons the Biblical model of *ecclesia*[18] - the gathering together of believers in Jesus Christ.

Popular Christian revisionist author Donald Miller sums up the thought process that many professing Christian millennials have adopted to excuse their habitual absence from gathering with the church:

> "So, do I attend church? Not often, to be honest. Like
> I said, it's not how I learn. But I also believe the church
> is all around us, not to be confined by a specific tribe.

---

[18] The New Testament was written primarily in Greek. This is the word translated 'church' and has the idea of congregating, gathering, or coming together for an observance of some sort.

I'm fine with where I've landed and finally experiencing some forward momentum in my faith. I worship God every day through my work. It's a blast."[19]

Miller and his devotees and many others who may have never heard of the guy but believe the same things seem to miss the whole point of church. It's not about you. It's not about how you learn. It's not about how you feel best able to 'connect' with God. Church is about Christ. Every Biblical local church is a part of the universal church which is the bride of Christ. It is all about Christ and, like it or not, is confined to the specific tribe of Christ and his followers exclusively. Sure, churches are to show love and care to all and should be welcoming and open places that offer the healing and hope found in Christ alone, but even this is not the primary point of church.

The primary point is to glorify and obey God in gathering together with others who profess faith in Christ, to stir one another up to love and good works and to remind one another that our hope is in Christ and He is coming again! Enjoying and worshipping God in your work or in nature or whatever it is you love most in life is certainly a part of the Christian life. To think, however, that enjoying God through nature or worshipping him through your work is an acceptable substitute for gathering in the local church for which Christ shed His blood is the definition of selfish and supercilious ignorance.

If you don't gather with God's people and say you 'worship God every day with your work' as your reason, you show very clearly that you and your work are idols more worthy of respect than Christ and his work as revealed in His word. Call yourself 'spiritual', but do not think you are

---

[19] Donald Miller, 'I Don't Worship God by Singing. I Connect with Him Elsewhere.' on Storylineblog.com

Holy Spirit-filled. Introduce yourself as a deist or believer in God, but please stop calling yourself a Christian. You have just as much right to that designator as someone who attends church every week but doesn't worship God in his life through the week. None.

"Ok. Maybe gathering together is important" you are thinking, "but must churches really sing? Don't you think it's a little weird and old-style?" Ephesians 5:19 and Colossians 3:16 show singing as a part of how we teach one another and show thanksgiving to God. "I just really struggle with leadership structures in the church." And yet Paul's letter to Titus shows very clearly that a healthy leadership structure is crucial to the functioning of a church and the history of the early church located in the New Testament book of Acts shows the importance of distinctions made between the different leadership offices for the effective operation of facilitating a healthy and relevant church community.

"Ok, but membership. I mean, is that really Biblical?" Call it what you will, but it is obvious that there were designators of 'belonging' and 'not belonging' in the local church (1 Corinthians 11:18-19) so yes, 'membership' and the words 'responsibility' and 'accountability' are fully Biblical. If you need further Biblical support for the importance of church, I point you to the 33 individual local churches referenced by name in the New Testament and the 6 regions where it is indicated there multiple local churches present. Coming together as a church for worship and reminder of the gospel (1 Corinthians 11, 15) was a core part of the New Testament believers' lives and is evident throughout church history. Have things been perfect? Far from it. Does everything that happens in church fill you with happiness? Probably not. There will be sadnesses and struggles in church just as in other parts of life, but in a Bible-based church you will find a family and friends, indeed a community, that you will not be able to find anywhere else.

No, church community doesn't exactly fit the selfie-style of the average millennial, but that is kind of the point. If a professing Christian millennial continues to follow the self-focused trend of his or her generation the reality is he or she is still at square one. In need of salvation in Christ that gives a heart and desire for service and sacrifice. As I have written elsewhere, 'The Christian life is not a beach on which to sleepily sun yourself. It is a battleground on which to sacrificial spend yourself.'

Chapter 4

Yes, words matter

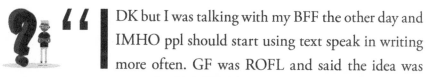

" DK but I was talking with my BFF the other day and IMHO ppl should start using text speak in writing more often. GF was ROFL and said the idea was OTT, but I feel like its text speak FTW."

Said no one ever.

Unless, perhaps,... a millennial (TBC).

Look, I get it. Many, maybe even most millennials suffer from FOMO. Its why our generation is constantly plugged in. True, some people's jobs and work situations mean having a smart-phone is wise and enables them to respond quickly to emails, messages, and to stay on top of certain admin responsibilities while on the go. At the same time, many are constantly on their devices where it can become quite clear that they are constantly anywhere but the place they actually are. You are having a meal with friends, but rather than chatting to the friends in front of your face you are chatting with your group on Facebook. You are having time to spend with your church family, but keep turning away to talk with your family elsewhere on Whatsapp and are clearly vacant from the conversation you were supposed to take part in. This becomes painfully obvious when you keep glancing at your device and responding with 'Yes', 'Really?' 'Hmmmm' and 'I see' with an inflection that reveals about as much interest in the other person as a pig takes in a smokehouse.

The examples go on, but I think you have the picture and it probably didn't elicit an LOL. And that's quite right because the increased abuse of words and proper vocabulary does have far reaching implications for education, intelligence, personal and spiritual growth, and the health of society.

When I see the sad decline of proper vocabulary and communication in my generation, I do smh. You may as well. At the same time those of us who do try to communicate in clear and universally understandable ways can find ourselves struggling with limited vocabulary and the over use of filler words and phrases. I'm trying to work on that myself and I ask other millennials to work hard in endeavouring to increase their vocabulary and intellectual capability. You may think it's NBD, but the evidence is to the contrary.

In trying to grapple with the challenge of teaching Medicine and other technical stuff to Millennials, Allan Platt gives the following not so glowing assessment:

> "...Millennials enter college with over 15,000 hours of television viewing and minimal plain-text reading time...They are very knowledgeable in their generational media, but lack knowledge in science, history, and

literature. They have problems constructing thoughtful paragraphs, instead splashing together random thoughts with limited vocabulary and lack of structure. Even though they are saturated with technology, their skills in research and workplace tasks are lacking."[20]

Back in the day (2010), England's first 'Communication Champion for Children', Jean Gross told *The Sunday Times* that the emerging teenagers of the Millennial generation were at risk of unemployment due to their lack of vocabulary, having a working vocabulary as low as 800 words. Michael McQueen notes

> "...in 1950 the average 14 year old had a vocabulary of over 25000 words in contrast to the average modern 14 year old whose vocabulary consists of just 10000 words."[21]

If only 10000 words were actually used.

Why all this faff about words? Why are they so important and should Christian millennials really care?

1. Words have precise meanings and precision in their usage and understanding is vital.

Words help us make sense of the world around us. Imagine a world without words. A world where there is no talking or conversation nothing to read, nothing to write, nothing to give signals of direction

---

[20] Allan Platt, PA-C, MMSc, 'Teaching Medicine to Millennials' in *The Journal of Physician Assistant Education* 2010 Vol 21 No 2

[21] Michael McQueen, The 'New' Rules of Engagement: A Guide to Understanding and Connecting with Generation Y, (Australia: NexGen Group Pty Ltd, 2007)

or danger. No sign language because there is no spoken language. A world without words would be more or less vegetative.

Communication in some form or another has always been key to the health of humanity. Even where communication with others is non-existent (if you've been stranded on an abandoned island for instance... or you've just chosen to remain at home all day), you are left to your thoughts, most of which are pictures and collections of words.

Given the crucial nature of words and language, it stands to reason that we take care to use words properly and appropriately. When we don't, we run risk of exaggeration and risk seeing words lose their proper understanding (e.g. whatever is 'awesome' is not very often, truly 'awesome'). While unintentional exaggeration can be understood many times as the positive fruit of some exuberant feeling and is often harmless, it can also be negative. This side of exaggeration generally comes out in day to day relationships. The words 'always' and 'never' are very broad terms that should only be used if the precise meaning applies. Generalisations are exaggerations that are often employed to make a point seem stronger.

We also run the risk of prevarication when we misuse words. We say 'Everything is O.K.' when actually things are not 'O.K.' This can lead to many problems. People assume honesty and so don't pursue what could be a helpful conversation with the less-than-transparent individual - they assume everything genuinely is 'O.K.' only to find out later that nothing was 'O.K.' Another problem is that when someone responds to the pleasantry of 'How are you?' and you respond 'I'm O.K. thanks', they may be so used to the expression being abused that they ask if anything is wrong. O.K. is no longer O.K.

I once engaged in a conversation in which I indicated that the Christian individual I was talking with was at *risk* of *appearing* [emphasis necessary] to be excusing some ongoing sin in her own life by defending something sinful. I was then accused of saying she *was* engaging in the sin which she was defending and was trying to excuse it. I had not said that at all. I spoke very precisely in pointing out the *risk* of *appearing* to be excusing a potential sin issue. Sadly, millennials often miss the important nuance of words and sentences and become defensive immediately, not stopping to think about the precise meaning of what has been said. They often hear what they want to hear or what they don't want to hear and question and attack anything that presents precise objective considerations.

Millennials, and for that matter anyone who struggles with precision in language, can learn some lessons from the Ancient Greeks. English can be a difficult language because it naturally can be far less precise than other languages. Consider the English word we often use, "love".

Our friend, Millennial Mike uses 'love' many times a day. Some examples:

"I love that new Ramen place."

"I loved *The Walking Dead* so much I watched the first few seasons in one week."

"I love my mom. She lets me stay rent and bill-free in her basement and buys all the groceries. She's awesome."

If Mike had a bit more responsibility, he may very well "love" his girlfriend or wife. Love, love, love. It's everywhere. But surely these are different types of love and surely "love" isn't the best word on some of the occasions Mike uses it to describe his emotions.

Eros, Philos, Sterge, and *Agape* are all precise Greek words that relate to a precise realm of our one word 'love'.

Eros, depicted in a famous statue at London's Piccadilly Circus, indicates romantic and erotic love, which when not in the context of marriage, more often than not is synonymous with lust. It is good and right for a husband and wife to have the passionate love of *eros,* but when not in that context, *eros* is impure.

Phileo denotes brotherly love and friendship. It is this concept on which the US city, Philadelphia gets its name and descriptor 'The city of brotherly love.' It is virtuous and is the love shared between equals.

Storge also denotes familial love, particularly that shown by a parent to a child.

Agape is the word that the New Testament uses to describe God's love for us. It is unconditional, and characterised by self-sacrificing devotion even when the recipient is undeserving and unlovable.

Reconsidering our use of certain words like "love" and assessing where we have diminished the beauty in the meaning by improper use of these words in conversation is important if we are to rescue them from meaninglessness and redeem them from their tarnished state. Be precise in how you speak and interpret others expecting the same precision.

2. Words indicate what is in a person's heart.

I believe not only in the authority of God's Word in speaking to and challenging us on real life issues (yes, even our trivial #firstworldprobs), I also believe it is sufficient and have never found it not to be so. With that in mind, seeing as how the Bible spends so much time talking about the tongue, I believe it is important to consider the Bible's words on how our words reflect our state before God. Here are some choice passages:

Proverbs 4.23-24 "Guard your heart above all else, for it is the source of life. Don't let your mouth speak dishonestly, and don't let your lips talk deviously."

Luke 6:45 "A good man produces good out of the good storeroom of his heart. An evil man produces evil out of the evil storeroom, for his mouth speaks from the overflow of the heart."

Matthew 12:34-35 "Brood of vipers! How can you speak good things when you are evil? For the mouth speaks from the overflow of the heart. A good man produces good things from his storeroom of good, and an evil man produces evil things from his storeroom of evil."

Mark 7:21-23 "For from within, out of people's hearts, come evil thoughts, sexual immoralities, thefts, murders, adulteries, greed, evil actions, deceit, promiscuity, stinginess, blasphemy, pride, and foolishness. All these evil things come from within and defile a person."

Millennial Mike objects:

> "This doesn't apply to swearing though. Swear words are just words. They're just expressive tools. They don't hurt anything and don't really matter. Besides they are more informed by culture than anything."

This is a typical reason I have heard excusing profanity, swearing, and just bog standard cussing. From the soft and seemingly innocuous millennial refrain of "OMG", it's spelled-out companion "Oh my God!", and the nonsensical "What the hell!?" to the more moderate "s***" to the very strong Fs and Cs to the blasphemous abuses of God's name in "God-d***" and "Jesus!", cussy exclamations not only fail to make logical sense, they do no good, regularly stir up anger and bitterness, and reflect a dark state of heart and mind.

Accepting such speech in your life or approving it in others' (including what you like and share on social media), is out of step with the holiness in which God call us to live. Still don't believe it's all that important for the Christian? Consider Ephesians 4:29, "No foul language is to come from your mouth..." and Colossians 3:8 that says if you are going to call yourself a Christian, you "must also put away all the following: anger, wrath, malice, slander, and filthy language from your mouth."

The language of which Paul writes is indeed applicable to our present day swear words and unwholesome, pointless, slang. Where such words are used or approved of there is bound to be the propensity to anger, malice, and slander - none of which are upbuilding and all of which are potentially devastatingly down-tearing as well as reflective of someone who is either immature in their faith or whose heart is not right at all with God.

3. Words can build up or tear down

If you happen to have an appropriate value for history you will be familiar with the background of the old saying "Loose lips sink ships".

During World War I there were many German spies who were employed to act as salesmen or just randoms on the street with the express intent of hanging around docks and listening out for any juicy morsels of information divulged by loose lipped people about shipping patterns. Many ships were sunk by German U-boats so it can only be assumed that some of these may likely have been due to "loose lips".

Indeed, the tongue has a remarkable capacity for wreaking havoc and destruction. So many times we feel like we want to say something or should say something when we should just zip it, put a lid on it, or in some other way shut our big fat mouths[22]

The Bible has a lot to say about the human tongue and the simultaneous dangers and delights it is capable of.

In Proverbs 13:3 we read that "The one who guards his mouth protects his life; the one who opens his lips invites his own ruin." Ecclesiastes 10:12 says, "The words from the mouth of a wise man are gracious, but the lips of a fool consume him." Hebrews 12:15 challenges churches to "Make sure that no one falls short of the grace of God and that no root of bitterness springs up, causing trouble and by it, defiling many."

James 3:3-12 dwells more fully on this subject and the constant battle we will have in seeking to tame our tongues and the very real indicator of hypocrisy that is the failure to do so. Meditate on these words:

> "Now when we put bits into the mouths of horses to make them obey us, we also guide the whole animal. And consider ships: Though very large and driven by fierce winds, they are guided by a very small rudder wherever the will of the pilot directs. So too, though the tongue is a small part of the body, it boasts great things. Consider how large a forest a small fire ignites. And the tongue is a fire. The tongue, a world of unrighteousness, is placed among the parts of our bodies. It pollutes the

---

[22] Please don't get depressed and think I'm calling you fat or make this book about 'fat-shaming' - that would be one of those exaggerations we've already addressed. It's a figure of speech. Chances are I don't know you or your weight and besides, I too have a fat mouth that sometimes needs to be shut!

whole body, sets the course of life on fire, and is set on fire by hell. Every sea creature, reptile, bird, or animal is tamed and has been tamed by man, but no man can tame the tongue. It is a restless evil, full of deadly poison. We praise our Lord and Father with it, and we curse men who are made in God's likeness with it. Praising and cursing come out of the same mouth. My brothers, these things should not be this way. Does a spring pour out sweet and bitter water from the same opening? Can a fig tree produce olives, my brothers, or a grapevine produce figs? Neither can a saltwater spring yield fresh water."

This pairs up with James' earlier challenge to "be slow to speak" and his assertion "If anyone thinks he is religious without controlling his tongue, then his religion is useless and he deceives himself." And yet, when our tongues are kept and conformed by the sanctifying work of the Holy Spirit we will be able to in any given situation say "what is good for building up someone in need, so that it gives grace to those who hear" as Ephesians 4:29 encourages us. What was good for the Ephesian church was also good for the Thessalonian church as Paul also told them to "encourage one another and build each other up as you are already doing" (1 Thessalonians 5:11).

This doesn't mean that words won't sting on occasion - indeed the truth often hurts initially - this is certainly true of many words in the Bible. Nevertheless, wise words that may poke and prod us are intended to steer and guide not hurt or harm. As Ecclesiastes 12:11 says "The sayings of the wise are like goads, and those from masters of collections are like firmly embedded nails. The sayings are given by one Shepherd."

4. Words are a tool through which we grow in knowledge and understanding of God, the world, and one another.

Think about it - God created words. It was with words that God created. Words are therefore both created and creative. We learn through words. We understand through words. We ask questions and get answers through words. We express ourselves through words or at the very least with words in mind.

Precision and accuracy is important for the sake of understanding one another properly - in any meaningful relationship, communication is key and words whether signed or spoken form a core part of communication. They can build up or they can destroy. From the serious to the sublime to the ridiculous, words help us relate to one another and play a vital role in facilitating understanding of who God is and who we are.

Language, being the beautiful thing that it is, furnishes us with words for those superficial conversations about obvious weather conditions ("What a messy day!"[23]), discussion about the more meaningful areas of sport, politics, literature, cinema, art, and other aspects of culture, and deliberation over deep issues of anthropology, philosophy, and theology. Within each of these fields, words provide us with context, content, and to some extent indicate, impact, and inform our conduct.

Without the words "holy", "mercy", "grace", "justice", "righteousness", "good", we would not be able to understand much at all about God or His interactions with mankind.

---

[23] Invariably spoken to an individual who is all too aware of the "messy day", having not utilised an umbrella.

Without the words, "identity", "personhood", "purpose", we would struggle to understand and respect one another in any way beyond an animalistic sense.

Without the words "depravity", "sin", "evil", "wickedness", "chaos", "mess", and "confusion", we would not have much ability to understand the core problems of humanity, perhaps spurring us to seek those things that are better. Without the words "redemption", "reconciliation", "justification", "sanctification", and "glorification" we might very well despair of finding hope, help, and healing in a beautiful world that we have broken.

Words have meaning; they are created and creative. We should strive to learn and understand even those words that initially are complex and difficult in their meanings so that we may better understand God, the world around us, and mankind. Through appreciating, understanding, and applying words properly we can be used by God to do much good. If you aren't that fussed, this is a simple challenge to get fussed. Words matter.

Chapter 5

Yes, History matters

 t is often said 'Those who do not study history are doomed to repeat it.'

Sadly, millennials are not only failing to study history or otherwise forgetting it (it is taught in some way in schools after all), we often fail to see the importance of history and so fail to process it practically.

Millennial music heartthrob, Harry Styles of *One Direction* fame, stars in Christopher Nolan's brilliant movie *Dunkirk*. The film tells the story of the Dunkirk evacuation (code-named Operation Dynamo) of trapped Allied Soldiers from the beaches and harbour of Dunkirk, France during World War II. When Styles' 1D fans heard the news, twitter was lit! Except that no one really knew what Dunkirk was about, one even asking "@HarryStyles what is a dunkirk?".

Another said how she hoped the movie was going to be 'fun'.

You heard correct ..."fun".

Last I checked "fun" was not a word that cropped up a lot in the WWII history books. Nor should it. Consider your response if someone asked "Have you heard the one about 9/11?" (I was once asked this…). Yeah. Not very fun or funny…but Dunkirk might be! *Face-palm*

The problem doesn't just extend to the ancient history that is World War II (reader, please note my sarcastic use of 'ancient' - WWII occurred in the middle of the last century and there are still many alive who witnessed it and even fought in it). In 2016 I went to the cinema to view the Mark Wahlberg film *DeepWater Horizon*. The film chronicles the well-known 2010 catastrophe that was the explosion of British Petroleum's *Deep Water Horizon* oil rig in the Gulf of Mexico. Many died and the livelihoods of many along the Gulf were severely affected. As I left the cinema, I overheard a conversation taking place behind me between two millennials in their late 20s.

"It was good, but it was a bit too much. I know it was supposed to be intense but…yeah, I don't know…it was a stand alone right or are they going to do another?"

I thought about turning around and saying "Pray God they don't have to do another. Don't you realise this was real??"

I managed to restrain myself.

What this sad ignorance showed me was that we are not only in danger of forgetting the important lessons from the distant past, we are also by and large unaware of the most recent of events and so see no correlation in consequences we may experience in the world today. Vital learning opportunities are lost and the tragedies of the past repeat themselves. And around and around we go.

If I had a £1 coin for every time I have sat talking with a fellow millennial about their education and been left with the sense that education is not valued I would be increasing in wealth. The amount of times where the scope is narrowed and I hear something like "I slept through history class. It was so boring." is very troubling.

Knowing the history of the past and being aware of history made in the present is not only a profitable endeavour in aiding one's intelligence, it should also be considered as part of a bigger picture of the universe's movement from A to Z. Implications of the past for the present and the way choices and actions of the past have impacted the present should be explored and attempts to understand them should be made. In this, one will discover that while time is linear, it often does appear to go in cycles.

Consider the words of Ecclesiastes 1:9-11:

> "What has been is what will be, and what has been done is what will be done, and there is nothing new under the sun. Is there a thing of which it is said, "See, this is new"? It has been already in the ages before us. There is no remembrance of former things, nor will there be any remembrance of later things yet to be among those who come after."

Remember the briefly quoted stat that millennials spend up to 18 hours a day consuming media? Well, most of that media is created by peers and doesn't extend much beyond the millennial generation.

Mark Bauerlein says

> "Young people have never been so intensely mindful of and present to one another, so enabled in adolescent

contact...The autonomy has a cost: the more they
attend to themselves, the less they remember the past
and envision a future...The fonts of knowledge are
everywhere, but the rising generation is camped in
the desert, passing stories, pictures, tunes, and texts
back and forth living off the thrill of peer attention.
Meanwhile, their intellects refuse the cultural and civic
inheritance that has made us what we are up to now."[24]

With little or no appreciation of history comes little or no appreciation
of primary sources and this is accompanied by a general ignorance as to
why certain beliefs and behaviours are present today. Without history it
is very easy to fall into a mindset that says every religion is equally right,
rules really don't matter as they are simply social constructs, structure
and organisation is overrated, and precision and politeness in language
really doesn't matter.

Given the lack of appreciation of history it is not hard to see why
#fakenews and alternative facts abound and interpretations of the
past equate to little more than historical revisionism without any real
grounding in concrete reality, villains becoming heroes and heroes
becoming villains.

In Christian circles, such revisionism is harming proper grounding
in the concrete truth of the Scriptures. Many are, perhaps cluelessly,
embracing a weird quasi-Christianity, inducing a sort of pseudo-
spirituality that sounds more like Oprah and Rob Bell's brand of new-
ageism than any God-breathed word of Scripture. The ideas that "we are

---

[24] Mark Bauerlein, *The Dumbest Generation: How the Digital Age Stupefies Young
Americans and Jeopardizes our Future, Or, Don't Trust Anyone Under 30*, (New York,
Jeremy Tarcher/Penguin, 2008), p 10

all in this together" and that "all paths lead to the top of the mountain" (whatever this means) may be nice thoughts, but they simply don't hold up logically or practically when confronted with facts.

Sadly, logic, facts, and objectivity are regularly discarded by millennials and replaced with irrational instinct, feelings, and subjectivity that throw discernment and discretion out the window. For the Christian reading the Quran, Buddhist Scriptures, or any religious text, commentary, or poetry included can be good and helpful to engaging with others. I actually encourage mature Christians to do this. Reading these, however, thinking there is actual guidance and truth to be gained from them is incredibly flawed and is incompatible with Christ's message of exclusivity.

Underlying this 'open-minded' brand of Christianity is a resentment of the hurt following Christ's call can bring, a reticence to trust the reality of the hope found in following His call, and a reluctance to accept the help found in following Christ alone. The historicity of pure Christianity is therefore doubted with the basic tenets of the faith redefined according to various individuals subjective and unique whims. Such doubts must be arrested and put to bed.

The Christian's hurt is historical

If you think that Christians have had it easier in the past consider Ecclesiastes 7:10 which challenges: "Don't say, "Why were the former days better than these?" since it is not wise of you to ask this." After meditating on this passage, pick up a book on church history. Read about all of the Christians who have given up everything to follow Christ. As you do, remember Christ's words to his disciples "If the world hates you, understand that it hated Me before it hated you." (John 15:18) and the promise "You will be hated by everyone…"(Matthew 10:22).

Inspiring stuff, right? And here you may have been thinking that being a Christian was something that was meant to make you feel warm and fuzzy inside and give you your best life now. Think again.

You may be asking why Christians are hated. Perhaps you think that you can get through the Christian life without experiencing other people's hatred. You may even think that those Christians who are hated are clearly doing something wrong or that earns them other people's hatred - fulfilling the Great Commission or something radical and provocative like that. Jesus tells his disciples that this hatred is on account of his name and is rooted in either ignorance of God's truth or proud ignoring of God's truth (John 15:21). It is not something you, as a Christian, will have to go looking for. It will be reality.

Genuine Christ-followers are well-acquainted with hurt. Consider Dietrich Bonhoeffer's words in *The Call of Discipleship*:

> "The cross is laid on every Christian. The first Christ-suffering which every man must experience is the call to abandon the attachments of this world. It is that dying of the old man which is the result of his encounter with Christ. As we embark upon discipleship we surrender ourselves to Christ in union with his death—we give over our lives to death. Thus it begins; the cross is not the terrible end to an otherwise god-fearing and happy life, but it meets us at the beginning of our communion with Christ. *When Christ calls a man, he bids him come and die.* It may be a death like that of the first disciples who had to leave home and work to follow him, or it may be a death like Luther's, who had to leave the monastery and go out into the world. But it is the same

death every time—death in Jesus Christ, the death of
the old man at his call."

While Bonhoeffer was primarily speaking of the ongoing need of the
Christian to die to sin, he was well acquainted with the reality that in
dying to sin and following Christ the Christian would gain enemies and
would experience suffering, mental, emotional, spiritual, and perhaps
even physical.

This suffering even to the point of death was experienced by Christ
himself. 10 of the 11 original apostles left after Judas' betrayal and
subsequent suicide would go on to live and be executed for their faith
in Christ.The same would be true of the later apostle, Paul whose letters
make up a significant chunk of the New Testament. A study of early
church history up til this point will show suffering and hurt experienced
directly as the result of open profession of faith in Christ has been pretty
standard across the globe. Both Peter and John write that we should
not be surprised when we suffer for Christ (1 Peter 4:12, 1 John 3:13).

If you read the Bible and then read history, the hurt you will experience
as a Christian will come as no surprise and you will be equipped with
examples of how to face it.

The Christian's hope is historical

With so much hurt, where is the hope? The hope is found in the hurt.
The Apostle Paul says in Romans 5:3-5

"...we rejoice in our sufferings, knowing that suffering
produces endurance, and endurance produces
character, and character produces hope, and hope does
not put us to shame, because God's love has been

poured into our hearts through the Holy Spirit who
has been given to us."

Saying goodbye to leaders of the church in Ephesus, Paul said that
he knew that he would encounter opposition and suffering in every
city he stepped foot in, but it didn't matter so long as he faithfully
completed the mission he was on to see Christ proclaimed (Acts 20:23-
24). Eventually, in what is chronologically Paul's last letter in the New
Testament, he indicates to Timothy that he knows his life is about to
end (he was eventually executed). And yet the hope which Paul had
remained and serves as an example of the goal which every Christian
should have in the words:

> "I have fought the good fight, I have finished the race,
> I have kept the faith. There is reserved for me in the
> future the crown of righteousness, which the Lord, the
> righteous Judge, will give me on that day, and not only
> to me, but to all those who have loved His appearing."
> (2 Timothy 4:7-8)

Remember Dietrich Bonhoeffer's words quoted in the last point?
Bonhoeffer was well acquainted with suffering as a Christian living in
and seeking to oppose the evils of Nazi Germany. He was just short
of 40 when on 9 April, 1945 he was marched naked to the gallows at
the Flossenburg concentration camp and hanged on order of Heinrich
Himmler. Two weeks later Flossenburg was liberated by U.S. troops and
one month later, Nazi Germany fell. Bonhoeffer's last words reflect his
fearlessness in death and the hope he had in Christ:

"This is the end, for me the beginning of life".

In January 1956, Nate Saint, Ed McCully, Jim Elliott, Roger Yoderian, & Peter Fleming were speared to death by the Waorani people in Ecuador who they were seeking to tell about Jesus. Elliot had once said "He is no fool who gives what he cannot keep to gain what he cannot lose."

Right before entering the jungle one last time, the "Ecuador Five" as some referred to them, sang a final hymn that reflected their hope. The final stanza of "We Rest On Thee" says:

"We rest on Thee, our shield and our defender!
Thine is the battle, Thine shall be the praise;
When passing through the gates of pearly splendor,
Victors, we rest with Thee, through endless days.
When passing through the gates of pearly splendor,
Victors, we rest with Thee, through endless days."

Such hope and such rest in Christ alone is a core part of the historical Christian faith. Hebrews 11:1 says: 'Now faith is the assurance of things hoped for, the conviction of things not seen.' (ESV). This faith begins with understanding God created the Universe as the Scriptures record it - and so we know all is in His control.

This faith continues to assure us of the validity of our hope through the example of countless men and women from the Old and New Testaments and through church history. Hope which whispers to us in the hurt we face and reminds us that we are not alone and that this world is not our home - Christ's new world is coming. Hope that reminds us in the words of the theologian Thomas Fuller (quoted by Harvey Dent in *The Dark Knight*) that 'The night is darkest just before the dawn'. Hope that sings 'In Christ alone, my hope is found, he is my light my strength my song.'

Sadly, many millennial professing Christians have forgotten that Christ alone gives hope. We have abandoned the historical orthodox Christian faith and have embraced something that looks more like Buddhism, Sufiism, or some home-made brand of Kabbalistic Jewish mysticism.

We might retweet a C.H. Spurgeon quote that says 'Without Christ, there is no hope', but we live more in the writings of Rumi and Rob Bell than we do Jesus Christ. We do this quite simply because it's cooler, easier, and less controversial. It is more satisfyingly universalistic than faithfully following and proclaiming Jesus and that hope of salvation from our arrogance, addictions, and alienation (our sin) really is in Him alone.

The Christian's help is historical

If Christian millennials start valuing history in general and take up an appreciation for church history in particular they will discover countless Christ-focused ways of being helped to hope when life really hurts. Certainly it is even this study of history which can be in itself a source of hope. Consider Romans 15:4:

> "For whatever was written in the past was written for our instruction, so that we may have hope through endurance and through the encouragement from the Scriptures."

1 Corinthians 11 1-12 also serves as a reminder of the way in which knowing history can help us do the right thing in the present when we have God's grace.

John Rippon, a hymn writer (author of *Hark the Herald Angels Sing* among others) was a pastor in London, England for 63 years of what would eventually be known as the Metropolitan Tabernacle. He spent much time in a cemetery known as Bunhill Fields. What would lead someone to spend time hanging out above dead people's bodies? Rippon valued history and spent time transcribing all of the names and epitaphs of Bunhill Fields' tombstones where so many heroes of nonconformist Christian faith are buried (look it up...Google exists for a reason). Through this exercise, Rippon was encouraged by the testimonies of faith and reminded of the hope in which so many before him had died and subsequently seen fulfilled. He didn't try to revision Christianity. He knew what it taught. He wasn't going to try to reinvent its teachings to make his hard task as a pastor in a difficult city easier. Rippon did his transcribing to consistently remind himself that he was not alone, others had gone before him, and a testimony of righteousness and legacy of peace was left for him to emulate.

It is with such an appreciation of history that you and I will be helped as we find our way through life's very real hurts, running on and fighting on to reach the hope we have in Christ alone.

Reinventing our own Christianity in practice may be possible. But it kills and ultimately damns. A personal reinvention of Christianity doesn't change the universal historical truth of who Christ was, what he stood for, why he came, and how he accomplishes our salvation. So while it may make you feel cooler to extract your theology from your fave quasi-spiritual fakely folk band, it's best to stick with the Bible and the consistent historical record of those who have believed in its truth.

Chapter 6

No, it is not right to 'question everything'

"Question everything."

This is the essence of "free-thinking" millennial ideology.

It is far from being exclusively a millennial problem - indeed, this is the attitude many millennials were raised to have by their parents. The problem is that this produces the syndrome that is "always learning and never able to arrive at a knowledge of the truth." (2 Timothy 3:7)

Asking questions is one thing. *Questioning everything* is quite another. Asking questions helps us understand and learn and has the goal of seeing us receive and accept factual answers. Admittedly, this goal, though possible, is not always reached, but that does not mean we stop seeking objective truth.

When the Christian, regardless of generation, looks to Christ and trusts in Christ, growing in His word, there is the desire to attain to full maturity in knowledge and understanding

> "...that we may no longer be children, tossed to and fro by the waves and carried about by every wind of doctrine, by human cunning, by craftiness in deceitful schemes." (Ephesians 4:14)

And yet it is the philosophy that says "Question everything" that leads to perpetual wandering. You wander from belief to belief. You wander from denomination to denomination, changing your views based purely on feelings and emotions. You wander from job to job. You wander from one interest to the next, never feeling satisfied. You wander from self-imposed modes of extreme boredom to overwhelming busy-ness and still are not satisfied.

You can't make decisions on the simplest of choices and the ideas of right and wrong are simply vague social constructs that will vary from one place to another and are defined purely by human convenience. Anytime someone makes a statement that sounds too objective or certain, you look for the cracks and holes wherein you can question, disprove, and dismantle. Your idea of discussion, looks a lot like intense and angry debate. You wonder why people drift away and don't really want to engage you on deep issues. It's a catch 22 for them though, because you then proudly assume that they are simpletons unable to engage on deep issues and in perhaps even "racist bigots" (this seems to be the easy way to dismiss those of different views these days).

You never consider that you are part of the problem. You never stop to think that perhaps people won't engage you on deeper issues because they don't want to find themselves in some kind of verbal version of WWE Smackdown where you've already staged your victory. You haven't considered that perhaps others are weary of being disagreed with on matters even that they know significantly more about. When things get real and hard and your subjective feelings are hurt, you do what our cowardly human nature generally does.

You run.

You wander.

Just because you "can't even" doesn't mean that understanding and solid answers are beyond your grasp and those of others.

Question because....old people.

For many millennials, old people - indeed anyone before the millennial generation - are past it. They don't have any appreciation for technology. They are almost dinosauric. Their ineptitude and simplicity in thinking coupled with their background of hard working and the standard that has set - makes old people irrelevant and a burden to society. It is no wonder that so many Millennials support legalisation of euthanasia. One random millennial blogger Emily Anderson says:

> "My generation, "the millennials", are stepping up to the plate to give the older generations of the United States a run for their money...We're chill because we are accepting and open to trying out new things whenever the time comes...It is important to have good morals and courage but the freedom to do as want with your life is just as important...I see euthanasia as an act of courage. I think of most of my generation also feels

this way. Because of this, I would consider myself a libertarian when it comes to thinking about euthanasia. Libertarians believe that justice comes through when the society is free to do whatever they please no matter the outcome…"

Let alone summing up every reason why I am not a libertarian, Emily unwittingly asserts that freedom to do whatever one wants with life is just as important as good morals - even when the freedom allows something immoral. Basically, freedom trumps morality. Imagine how much more messed up our society would be with this mentality that logically and consistently must say "anything goes."

The amount of condescension and patronisation shown to the genuinely elderly can be truly disturbing. Baby talk, unnecessarily raised volume with a different voice, and endless presumptions show a lack of respect for those with more life experience, who have often lived with far more contentment with far less. Millennials, however, often see the elderly as irrelevant, ignorant, and with little to offer. In some ways this probably has been true of other generations in their attitude to the elderly, but the latent disregard for the elderly among millennials truly seems to know no bounds.

This is often parodied in popular culture. In season 5, episode 11 of *The Simpsons*, Homer Simpson's dad asks to help find a local cat burglar. In front of many representatives of Springfield, Homer responds: "Sorry Dad. You've done a lot of great things. But you're a very old man now. And old people are useless."

In the American version of *The Office* Michael Scott asks with a degree of incredulity "So older people have just as many rights as younger people?." He then goes on to parody the type of treatment the elderly get when leading an ageism awareness seminar, asking "Why do we as a society hate old people so much?" Michael gets the response from one man "Because they're lame". What follows for many is a painfully familiar scenario, where the stereotype of funny, story telling old people is upheld as the primary reason to respect the aged. An elderly founder of the company, Dunder Mifflin, is brought in to inspire the office with some stories of the past. Michael quickly wearies of the man and unceremoniously ushers him out of the room. Its funny on TV, but it's all too familiar for some.

The Bible certainly does not have such a low view of the elderly. It challenges the GenY's tendency to listen only to peers. Take a break from reading this and look up Solomon's son Rehoboam and how he only listened to his buddies when making a crucial decision for the Kingdom of Israel. It didn't go well for Rehoboam or for Israel.

Basic honour and respect shown in simple ways are important. Leviticus 19.32 says, "You are to rise in the presence of the elderly and honor the old. Fear your God; I am Yahweh."

Yes, manners matter - even if no one else shows them.

Listening and paying attention to the elderly out of respect and a desire to learn is important. Proverbs 16.35 says "Gray hair is a glorious crown." and later on in Proverbs 23.22 the reader is in a more specific way charged, "Listen to your father who gave you life, and don't despise your mother when she is old."

"But they can't do the most basic stuff on an Iphone."

Yeah. They 've done more and accomplished more without an Iphone than you and I ever could with one. They used their brains and brawn to accomplish things. We use modern technology, which is fallible, to do our thinking and working for us. With far more, we so often accomplish far less.

Job 12.12 sagely notes "Wisdom is found with the elderly, and understanding comes with long life." 1 Timothy 5:1 encourages us "Do not rebuke an older man, but exhort him as a father." On this basis, questioning, ignoring, or lacking patience with a person simply because they are old, you don't think they can relate to you, and you believe they are "past it" is way is out of line. You may think that your way is better than an old way - but that doesn't give you license to disrespect and discard God's way of treating your elders with respect, courtesy, and patience.

Question because...conspiracy.

The problem with questioning everything is not only recognised by Christians, and is discarded philosophically with great ease through the simple use of logic. Brian Dunning, a science writer and producer of the *Skeptoid* weekly podcast gives three tests by which one should assess whether something should be questioned these being: 1) Is it ridiculous? 2) Is it axiomatic? And 3) Has it already been questioned to death? Dunning observes what is perhaps one of the more frustrating aspects of 'questioning everything' in regard to conspiracy theories. He notes,

> "...where I hear "Question everything!" the most is in cases where a popular belief runs counter to mainstream science or history. It is the rallying cry of the conspiracy

theorist, the revisionist historian, the alternative science crank. They attack science with an ad-hominem against who promotes it rather than what it actually means. 9/11 was an inside job because the government says it wasn't; you can run your car on water because the gasoline companies say you can't; crystals heal cancer because Big Pharma says they don't."[25]

I have had the displeasure of sitting through conversation upon conversation that casually made mention of bizarre theories, presenting them as fact. I have not quite had the experience of chatting with one of the 12 million Americans who believe the world is ruled by shape-shifting lizard people,[26] but it's only a matter of time I suppose.

Many of the conversations I have had featured fairly intelligent individuals, many of whom profess to be Christians. On some occasions I have laughingly joked about Illuminati theories and the paranoia of many in regard to virtually any function of civilised society, particularly those whose branding includes anything vaguely triangular. Let's just say that I shouldn't have joked about it. There are probably some people who now live under the delusion that obscure and insignificant Regan is a part of this quest for world-wide domination. A mole for the Masons. A hatchetman of the New World Order. I am not.

More common conspiracies in churches are over Bible translations, music, and the acceptability of entertainment in a Christian's life. Many are suspicious of any Bible translation that is not the Authorised

---

[25] Brian Dunning, No, You Shouldn't Question Everything, *Skeptoid Podcast*, August 2, 2016
[26] Philip Bump, '12 Million Americans Believe Lizard People Run Our Country' in *The Atlantic,* 2 April, 2013

(also known as King James) Version. Thanks to YouTube previously and mercifully confined rantings of independent fundamentalists like Stephen Anderson are now available across the world enabling a millennial and UK resident Bulgarian acquaintance married to a Chinese lady to adopt faulty, last century, and uniquely American theological ideas.

As for music, I have heard it said that anything that can be accompanied with a drum and guitar is not worthy of God and can be classified as 'beats of Beelzebub'. A previous millennial member of my church who craved conspiracy - essentially concluded that hymn writer Stuart Townend was only serving God for personal gain because a local concert charged a token fee for entry to cover costs and expenses.

Others decry anything entertaining as sinful and as part of a Satanic conspiracy to distract us by those things that we find enjoyable. One man confessed to me in an apologetic tone that his children had been mostly playing on that day "and...well...we try not to do too much of that really as play isn't very profitable." I do not desire to give this segment any more paper space as it is giving voice to the delusions of paranoia and fake piety.

Does the Bible really address this issue of conspiracy in any direct and practical way? You bet it does. Let's once again let it speak for itself.

In Titus 3:9, Paul tells us to 'avoid foolish controversies, genealogies [placing spiritual significance on names and numbers], dissensions, and quarrels about the law, for they are unprofitable and worthless.' (ESV)

1 Timothy 1:4 has Paul challenging Timothy to "remain at Ephesus so that you may charge certain persons not to teach any different doctrine,

nor to devote themselves to myths and endless genealogies [emphasis added], which promote speculations rather than the stewardship from God that is by faith.

Again, in 1 Timothy 4:7 Paul says, "Have nothing to do with irreverent, silly myths. Rather train yourself for godliness..."

Paul lays down the smackdown in 1 Timothy 6:4, "If anyone teaches another doctrine and disagrees with the sound words of our Lord Jesus Christ and with godly teaching, he is conceited and understands nothing. Instead, he has an unhealthy interest in controversies and semantics, out of which come envy, strife, abusive talk, evil suspicions, and constant friction between men of depraved mind who are devoid of the truth." (Berean Study Bible)

In 2 Timothy 2:14 Paul once more tells Timothy to challenge his congregation "not to fight about words; this is in no way profitable and leads to the ruin of the hearers."

Finally, 2 Timothy 2:23 says, "Have nothing to do with foolish, ignorant controversies; you know that they breed quarrels."

It would seem that Paul had all too much experience with people whose questioning spirits and craving for controversy were destructive to churches and portrayed constant and clear distraction from the big picture - the Gospel of Jesus Christ. I also really feel for Timothy who seems to have been surrounded by people who had serious issues with craving controversy and looking for significance in the trivial.

For Paul, controversial topics (note well that this does not include matters of Godly morality that for Paul were not controversial) and conspiracy theories were stupid and showed a lack of good stewardship of time and resource while also being poisonous to local church unity and strength. I am all too aware of the ridiculous debates and controversies that Christians can be sucked into. They must be avoided at all costs.

Question because...money

"Money and the rich are to blame for almost everything wrong in today's society. Indeed, it would seem that 'the establishment' and 'the elite' are all part of a sinister and sadistic plot to perpetuate poverty. No one who is rich came by money honestly and they certainly don't use their riches honourably. And it stands to reason. Money is the root of all evil, right?"

Such questioning of society on the basis of income and wealth inequality is standard among millennials.

Certainly, there are important issues to consider and, in some areas, address in regards to money. That said questioning honesty, validity, or integrity on the basis of money or how much something costs is simply not helpful or conducive to being a good citizen.

The best way of tackling this matter is to address the idea that "money is the root of all evil".

Let me play Captain Obvious for a moment.

The same people who think this have some money - however much or little themselves. You have to have money to buy food, pay your rent or mortgage, hand over your taxes, and pay your insurance, let alone countless other areas of both necessity and luxury. Is money then really the root of all evil? Surely there are some sins you have committed, some evil actions you have done, that had nothing to do with money?

So that means the Bible is not accurate or is generalising when it says 'Money is the root of all evil' then, right? No. Such a verse is not found in the Bible.

1 Timothy 6:10 says that "it is the love of money which is the root of all kinds of evil."

Often times money has nothing to do with the evils in our society. Rape, sexual immorality, and murder in many cases, perhaps most, do not have anything to do with money.

Elsewhere, in Ecclesiastes 5:10 we read "He who loves money is never satisfied with money and whoever loves wealth is never satisfied with income. This too is futile." Some of Jesus' words on the matter are recorded in Matthew 6:24 "No one can be a slave of two masters, since either he will hate one and love the other, or be devoted to one and despise the other. You cannot be slaves of God and of money." The unknown author or preacher of Hebrews says "Your life should be free from the love of money. Be satisfied with what you have, for He Himself has said, I will never leave you or forsake you." (Hebrews 13:5).

Money in and of itself is just a thing and cannot itself be sinful. The attitude behind earning money and how it is kept and spent, however, can be. Being rich is not the problem, how one experiences and uses their riches can be however. Paul writes:

> Instruct those who are rich in the present age not to be arrogant or to set their hope on the uncertainty of wealth, but on God, who richly provides us with all things to enjoy. Instruct them to do what is good, to be rich in good works, to be generous, willing to share,

storing up for themselves a good reserve] for the age to come, so that they may take hold of life that is real. (1 Timothy 6:17-19)

Often the skepticism behind those who are wealthy and the questioning of anything or anyone with money stems more from jealousy and envy. Millennials struggle with entitlement and this, coupled with laziness and love of free stuff, leads to questioning when things cost more than desired or aren't free. It is no wonder then that so many millennials are drawn to communism and socialism's promises. With the previously discussed lack of appreciation for history, lessons that could be learned from last century's communist conundrums fade into irrelevance.

Question because...religion

To the average millennial religion is about totalitarianism, money (as above), and control. Anything religion touches it taints. If money isn't the root of all evil in the world then religion is. We are told that religion has started more wars than anything else. Anything to do with religion should always be questioned. Such sweeping statements are standard in the West's increasingly anti-God environment, but are these statements substantiated and is questioning everything that has anything to do with religion important?

Let's first discard the idea that religion is the root of all evil and the root of all wars. Sam Harris, prominent atheist author calls faith and religion 'the most prolific source of violence in our history.'[27] This is a very charged statement but is curious given an analysis of war throughout human history. In Philip and Axelrod's *Encyclopedia of Wars*, 1,763 wars

---

[27] Sam Harris, *The End of Faith: Religion, Terror, and the Future of Reason* (Free Press, 2006), 27

have been listed as taking place throughout human history. Only 123 of these were religious in nature, 66 of these waged in the name of Islam.[28]

This is perhaps the first time 7% has been considered a majority.

Assessing the 20th century alone, a grim picture of power is formed in which atheistic nationalism, socialism, and communism can be directly linked to the massacring of up to 360 million people. So that's the idea that religion is the root of all evil busted.

But what of those wars and conflicts and problems that are due to religion? It cannot be argued that there are no issues for sure. It is here where actually saturating oneself in the source material is crucial. Assessing historical reliability and veracity is vital. When this is done seriously, we are left to consider the claims of essentially three monotheistic religions, Judaism, Christianity, and Islam. These three make what may appear to some to be similar claims, but they are fundamentally different. Rather than questioning everything and answering nothing, thereby unwittingly embarrassing yourself, why not do your own study of the primary sources? If you want to actually talk about this with the goal to learn and understand why not get in touch with me? I will try to steer you in the right direction.

The underlying problems

A questioning spirit is not the root or source of millennials' problems. If only it were. Sadly, the reality is far darker and much harder to deal with.

There are three words that I believe sum up the sin issue at the root of a questioning spirit: pride, presumption, and prejudice.

---

[28] Charles Phillips and Alan Axelrod, *Encyclopedia of Wars,* (Facts on File, 2004)

A questioning spirit is the fruit of **pride** because it refuses to trust, rejects any answer given, and insists on being contraire in everything.

Consider the format of a discussion between an average Millennial (yes, I have specific people in mind) and someone else.

The millennial will make a case and will question or be contraire when that case is contradicted in some way. Eventually though, the other person sees that the millennial is right at least in some way and agrees. The millennial could very well change tack at that point and find something else within the discussion where there is still likely disagreement. Unity and love in the disagreement is off the cards.

I have seen it. Perhaps, at times, I have been guilty of it. In such cases, pride is evident. Sadly in many cases, the underlying **presumption** by the questioning individual is that there will be no eventual unity in thought and that the debate will be a point of division or difference with which one can happily and legitimately take offence (seriously guys, you can take offence too much - it's like many of us are addicted to being offended). The presumption (and in some twisted sense, perhaps even the desire) that no agreement will be made is often accompanied by a **prejudiced** attitude against the other individual. This prejudice takes different forms.

Sometimes pride, presumption and prejudice is racial. "He's white." "He's black." "She's a refugee." "She's American and not British so can't understand us British." "He's British not American so can't understand us and our culture." "He's Nigerian, so...enough said."

I've heard all the racially prejudiced and proud presumptions I care to hear in this life and experienced some myself (no it's not just a black/

white issue). There is no room for this in the body of Christ. From one man, God made all nations (Acts 17:26).

Other times pride, presumption, and prejudice is generational. "He's just a crappy old man...don't pay him any mind." "She's clearly slipping mentally, it's probably best not to sit and talk with her." "He's too young and naive."

It can be socio-economical. "What a toff. I can't really trust anything he says or his motives...I mean he openly claims to being a Tory even!" "Does he have a job? I question whether I can trust or have a legitimate discussion with someone who is likely on benefits...I mean, there must be a reason he is on hard times."

Friends, the Bible's call to avoid any partiality (read the Letter of James), cuts both ways. In many cases pride, presumption, and prejudice is simply borne out of a developed hatred for what is good, right, and true and the need to sear one's conscience to live comfortably in that hate.

C.S. Lewis addresses these skeptics and habitual questioners in *The Abolition of Man* saying quite aptly:

> "Their scepticism about values is on the surface: it is for
> use on other people's values; about the values current in
> their own set they are not nearly sceptical enough."[29]

Stop questioning. Start answering. Come out of your enslavement to doubt and your dangerous free-spirit ideology. Start resting in objective and concrete truth.

---

[29] C.S. Lewis, *The Abolition of Man*, (New York: Macmillan Publishing, 1955), 41

Chapter 7

No, you are not promised an 'awesome' and easy life

e warned. This chapter may be the hardest with which to come to terms. Certainly some millennials when confronted with the realities discussed herein will be left feeling as lost as a ball in high weeds (not very good). Sorry, not sorry (or soz not soz...if you prefer). You are not the only person having to deal with harsh realities in this life and your self assessed personal merit is not taken into consideration by the course of the fallen world we live in.

So while this chapter may leave you feeling in need of a visit to the local "wellness centre" or cause you to google "dirt cheap yoga retreat", I assure you, you and I need to be honest about the reality that doing what's good and right in as much as we are able on a regular basis does not necessarily lead to smooth sailing and prosperity in life. If this idea is already leaving you feeling hot under the collar, may I advise contemplating this chapter's title in prayer while reading Job, Psalms, Proverbs, Ecclesiastes, the gospel accounts, Acts, and 2 Corinthians

11-12. This exercise will do a lot more for you than cooling down at the nearest artisanal juice and water bar, I assure you.

Selfie-Syndrome

Stats from 2015 revealed that there were more selfie-related deaths than shark related deaths with a figure comparable to skate-boarding deaths.[30] Accidents and life-threatening occurrences linked to selfie-taking are all too commonly reported in the news. The stats from 2015 also revealed that of the selfie-related deaths none of the victims were over the age of 32. Certainly not everyone who takes a selfie is irresponsible or risking life and limb. Though I am not a fan of selfies, I do occasionally take one, particularly if with someone else who is keen. I am not bashing the occasional taking of selfies - I do, honestly, want to bash what I am going to call 'selfie-syndrome', known formally as 'narcissism.'

So...narcissism. You know it right? Perhaps not. The term refers to a story in one of those crusty old books on Greek mythology that you chose not to read because you saw Disney's Hercules, the Percy Jackson movies (you may have or may have not been aware that these were based on books), and Troy. Narcissus was full of himself, his life and above all his beauty. No one who loved him was worthy of him in his mind and his pride and disdainful attitude were his ultimate downfall. In short, Narcissus was drawn to a pool of water, fell in love with his own reflection, couldn't tear himself away, and subsequently lost the will to live.

Sound familiar? It is only a slightly different story to that of so many millennials today. Think about it for a moment. It's true.

---

[30] Helena Horton, 'More people have died by taking selfies this year than by shark attacks' in *The Daily Telegraph*, 22 September 2015

In an at times blistering piece cover piece in *Time*, Joel Stein writes:

> "The incidence of narcissistic personality disorder is nearly three times as high for people in their 20s as for the generation that's now 65 or older, according to the National Institutes of Health; 58% more college students scored higher on a narcissism scale in 2009 than in 1982. Millennials got so many participation trophies growing up that a recent study showed that 40% believe they should be promoted every two years, regardless of performance. They are fame-obsessed: three times as many middle school girls want to grow up to be a personal assistant to a famous person as want to be a Senator, according to a 2007 survey; four times as many would pick the assistant job over CEO of a major corporation. They're so convinced of their own greatness that the National Study of Youth and Religion found the guiding morality of 60% of millennials in any situation is that they'll just be able to feel what's right. Their development is stunted..."[31]

Stein goes on to note the natural product of narcissism, 'entitlement'. This relates to the idea of certain rights that one feels they have...which they actually don't. An entitlement complex is generally reflected in the mindset that feels it has the right to enjoy life in every way. Enjoyment and pleasure become gods to the one suffering from an entitlement complex. What is unenjoyable is not worthwhile. What is hard is unnecessary and should be given up. What is challenging, convicting, or calls for personal change should be ignored.

---

[31] Joel Stein, 'The Me Me Me Generation' in *Time,* 20 May, 2013

Stats show that more and more young people, primarily millennials suffer from an entitlement complex. Dr. Joshua Grubbs who has presented some of these stats in a study describes the danger of entitlement saying,

> At extreme levels, entitlement is a toxic narcissistic trait, repeatedly exposing people to the risk of feeling frustrated, unhappy and disappointed with life.
>
> Often times, life, health, ageing and the social world don't treat us as well as we'd like.Confronting these limitations is especially threatening to an entitled person because it violates their worldview of self-superiority.[32]

Do you suffer from an entitlement complex? Here is a checklist:

- ❒ Do you frequently disregard rules or change them to suit yourself?
- ❒ Do you freeload (remember to be brutally honest)?
- ❒ Do you inconvenience others regularly with lack of punctuality, unreasonable requests, or presuming on others' generosity?
- ❒ Do you like to be seen and heard as the leader? Do you think your opinion is best? Do you question anyone and everyone else you feel disagrees with you?
- ❒ Do you like to talk about your own achievements and promote yourself?
- ❒ Do you ever have the 'I am special' chat with yourself in front of a mirror?
- ❒ Do you justify yourself when you do something that is wrong?

---

[32] J. B. Grubbs and J. J. Exline, Trait entitlement: A cognitive-personality source of vulnerability to psychological distress. Psychological Bulletin, 142(11), 1204-1226. (2016)

Yes? Then you are entitled and your relationships with others are in serious jeopardy.[33] Your relationship with God is more likely than not non-existant.

An entitlement complex sees the affected person unsettled and free in the worst sense possible - there is no anchor, no mooring, no understanding of reality and life's sometimes hard and harsh realities.

If you aren't enjoying your job, give it up. If you don't enjoy your living accommodation, give it up. If you don't enjoy your family life, run away. If you don't enjoy your study, just quit. If you don't enjoy some aspects of your marriage, get divorced. If you don't enjoy something about your church, just leave. You are entitled to enjoyment, pleasure, and ease. Be free. Follow your dreams. Do what you want. Don't be tied down by social constructs and ridiculous religious expectations. Don't be told what to do. Go on. Be a rebel....ruin your life if you want. It's your life after all and it doesn't matter how your actions may affect others. Such seems to be the mindset of many millennials.

Whether you 'feel' entitled or not, perhaps you should look at some key Millennial behavioural traits noted by Alex Bitterman in summing up college and university educators' perception of Generation Y and ask if they are true of you.[34]

1. Millennials are prone to very public complaining
2. Millennials are too emotional voicing their worries and concerns rather than taking a risk and "jumping in" to a task.

---

[33] Alice Boyes Ph.D, '9 Types of Entitlement Tendencies and How to Overcome Them' in Psychology Today (04 March, 2013)

[34] Alex Bitterman Ph.D, The College Question: Why college (as we know it) isn't working for The Millennial generation (Buffalo, New York: Balanne and Co. Press, 2013), 19

3. Millennials have few reservations about questioning those in authority.
4. Millennials are informal and do not respect hierarchy or social structure.
5. Millennials want to be overachievers, but not necessarily work to achieve their goals (millennials want things "handed to them")

It is increasingly less surprising that millennials are often referred to as 'Generation Me'. Whether you think this is a fair or accurate descriptor or not doesn't matter, somehow this *has* been the perception of and aura that surrounds many millennials and that *does* matter. This perception needs to change, but it won't unless millennials change. This change starts with you. Sure, it calls you to abandon your entitlement-borne delusion that every facet of your life should be as awesome as you make it seem on Facebook.

Going beyond that we need to accept the lie we have bought that we we are entitled to empowerment.

Oz all over again

Are you familiar with the story of *The Wonderful Wizard of Oz*? The book and film's namesake is billed by his subjects and those familiar with him as a great and powerful wizard. Such is his power and the greatness of his city that residents believe all who enter the city gates must wear emerald tinted spectacles lest they be blinded by the city's brilliance. In the course of the story, the great and powerful Oz is revealed to be not quite so great and powerful - he is actually a rather diminutive man and very average, but has built up a very realistic image of power that hides his very real weaknesses.

The story of Oz is in many ways a parable of the millennial complex as much as that of Narcissus. We crave empowerment. Whatever it looks like, whatever it means, however it is defined. Throughout the history of man self empowerment has been a primary motive that has guided our thoughts and actions. Indeed it was the idea of empowerment that man was sold in Genesis 3 by the serpent. Check it out.

> "Now the serpent was the most cunning of all the wild animals that the Lord God had made. He said to the woman, "Did God really say, 'You can't eat from any tree in the garden'?" The woman said to the serpent, "We may eat the fruit from the trees in the garden. But about the fruit of the tree in the middle of the garden, God said, 'You must not eat it or touch it, or you will die.'" "No! You will not die," the serpent said to the woman. "In fact, God knows that when you eat it your eyes will be opened and you will be like God, knowing good and evil." Then the woman saw that the tree was good for food and delightful to look at, and that it was desirable for obtaining wisdom. So she took some of its fruit and ate it; she also gave some to her husband, who was with her, and he ate it. Then the eyes of both of them were opened, and they knew they were naked; so they sewed fig leaves together and made loincloths for themselves."

You see it, right? If you read the rest of Genesis 3 you will understand that the world is in the mess it is in because of this one act of lusting for 'empowerment'.

In trying to be like God, we became thoroughly ungodly and have gravitated to making our own standard the measure of good and evil. Basically, we have made ourselves our own gods. We find strength in self. We find fulfillment in personal successes. We want to see ourselves lifted up. We want prosperity, happiness, and success and believe for some reason that these are all human rights regardless of whether we live responsibly or irresponsibly. There is no sense of accountability or acceptance of culpability for the problems we experience or the problems that are in the world. We are proud, selfish, externally passionate and overly confident, but internally insecure and troubled because we know the truth - we are living a lie.

Feels bad man

Perhaps you are feeling a little hurt right now. While you have been reading this book, you may have formed the idea that you don't really like me, which is ok and I assure you puts you in a camp inhabited by many others.

That said, if you are truly "open-minded" and a "free-thinker" by definition you should consider and test yourself on the validity of mine and other people's observations of millennials problems. In honesty, if this book and the contents of this chapter so far have made you feel bad and in need of a safe space, this may well be simply a sense of your conscience informing you of the need to get sorted. Here are some foundational truths that will help point us to the right path away from the sins of our self-serving narcissism, entitlement, and empowerment.

This world is not good - God is good.

The world is far from safe. That should be fairly obvious. Problems abound and there is constant lack of peace. Millennials know this. While there can often be a lack of responsibility accepted for the problems in the world and one will scarcely hear a millennial say 'I'm sorry', millennials do see the reality that things are not right in the world. Millennials do desire shelter and safety from the wrong in the world. If only the attempt to find this shelter and safety didn't rest in the shallow security offered by pre-defined safe-spaces.

David Livingstone, a bold and dedicated explorer and missionary put it well: 'There is one safe and happy place, and that is in the will of God.' This is because while the world and its people - including you and me - are not good, God is good. Read the Bible and you will quickly become aware of these realities.

This world is not God - God is God.

We see the problems in the world and are all too familiar with it's people's problems, but so often we act as though the world is God. We do this by submitting ourselves to every cultural fad and societal trend. Whatever is popular with the world becomes the standard by which we judge what is right and wrong. We fear what people think or what they will say about us if we do something different. We are people-pleasers. We crave popularity. We allow ourselves to be slotted into different categories and allow ourselves to be branded and defined by our generational characteristics as expected by the world around us.

Romans 12:2 challenges us "Do not be conformed to this world, but be transformed by the renewal of your mind, that by testing you may discern what is the will of God, what is good and acceptable and perfect." If you are a Christian, stop acting like the world is your God. Stop acting like the world knows best. Stop being defined by society's low expectations. Strive to please God and do His will. Care about what he says over anyone else. As John Bunyan put it 'What God says is best, is best, though all the men in the world are against it.'

This world is not glory-granting - God is glorious and glory-granting

As much as you try to feel empowered and empower others you will consistently find yourself feeling anything but strong. You will find that life doesn't hand out participation trophies and the glory that you get is soon snuffed out. Whatever trophies, wealth, riches, or success you get in this life, it will never truly satisfy and its glory will fade as life itself. You are not entitled to any good or glory in this life. Consider Ecclesiastes 9:11

> "Again I saw that under the sun the race is not to the swift, nor the battle to the strong, nor bread to the wise, nor riches to the intelligent, nor favor to those with knowledge, but time and chance happen to them all."

A passage that kicks entitlement in the teeth if ever there was one.

Rather than focusing on yourself consider a better attitude which is that outward focus exemplified in Christ.

> "Have this mind among yourselves, which is yours in Christ Jesus, who, though he was in the form of God, did not count equality with God a thing to be grasped, but emptied himself, by taking the form of a servant, being born in the likeness of men. And being found in human form, he humbled himself by becoming obedient to the point of death, even death on a cross. Therefore God has highly exalted him and bestowed on him the name that is above every name, so that at the name of Jesus every knee should bow, in heaven

and on earth and under the earth, and every tongue confess that Jesus Christ is Lord, to the glory of God the Father." (Philippians 2:5-11)

Where real power lies

For the Christian, strength and glory is found in God's strength and glory upon recognising our own weakness and frailty. If allowed to pick favourite Bible passages, I have to say that Isaiah 40 is on up there. When multiple shoulder dislocations and two surgeries ended my promising Basketball career before anyone knew it was promising or a potential career,[35] I found Isaiah 40 a reminder of my own life's trivialities and God's surpassing greatness. When I was suffering from myocarditis and spent two weeks in bed followed by months of attempting to regain lost fitness I turned to Isaiah 40 again. When struggling with balancing work, study, and ministry responsibilities and necessities I have turned to Isaiah 40. When difficulties have threatened unity and peace in the local church I help pastor, I have turned to Isaiah 40. When my wife left me one evening and I saw her the next day with another man, it was not long before yet again I turned to Isaiah 40 as I mourned the loss of one I loved and whom I thought loved me. When a friend and fellow Christian labourer was killed in an accident in front of me on a mission to Iraq, I turned to Isaiah 40. When that path saw me begin exploring marriage with my friend's daughter, in my joy at God's gracious providence, I turned to Isaiah 40.

In day to day struggles, I continue to preach these words to myself. Why? It reminds me that I will fall and fail in my own strength. And that is ok, because as a Christian it teaches me that my own strength is nothing. It humbles. It points me to the glorious God who pick us up

---

[35] Trust me…it was promising…no one else knew it though… #alternativefacts

and carries us in His own strength. It is for these reasons that we fall, that we may rely totally on our Saviour. In the words of old Authorised Version (KJV) from which I first learned this passage:

> "Hast thou not known? hast thou not heard, that the everlasting God, the Lord, the Creator of the ends of the earth, fainteth not, neither is weary? there is no searching of his understanding.He giveth power to the faint; and to them that have no might he increaseth strength. Even the youths shall faint and be weary, and the young men shall utterly fall: But they that wait upon the Lord shall renew their strength; they shall mount up with wings as eagles; they shall run, and not be weary; and they shall walk, and not faint." (Isaiah 40:28-31)

A closing word

I have written this book with no regrets. I have tried to be straightforward, clear, evidence based, and faithful to the Bible's teaching. Forgive me if in any of these areas I have fallen short and so failed to achieve the book's primary objective.

I have written in the hope that my fellow millennials will respond better to myself as a member of this generation than perhaps they would if this material came from someone else. Some of what I have said may have been tough and not appreciated. Sometimes what we need in life is a good kick up the backside and a good coach who loves us and cares for us getting up in our face telling it to us like it is.

This Earth already has one to many wusses. Please stop adding to the problem and start setting a better example for the next generation.

Don't waste your youth. Work hard. Live boldly. Love deeply. Take God-glorifying risks in faith. Speak the truth. Always put God and His people first. Be disciplined. Value the lessons of the past. Root yourself in concrete answers. Don't expect it to all be easy, but look to Christ for peace that lets you sleep in the bottom of life's boat in the middle of the world's howling storms.

As a child I grew up with Godly parents who prayed for and with me and sang songs that, while simple engrained principles of truth in me from a young age.

This little light of mine
I'm gonna let it shine
This little light of mine
I'm gonna let it shine
This little of mine
I'm gonna let it shine
Let it shine, let it shine, let it shine.

Shine all over Tumbling Shoals I'm gonna let it shine
Shine all over Tumbling Shoals I'm gonna let it shine
Shine all over Tumbling Shoals I'm gonna let it shine
Let it shine, let it shine, let it shine.

Well, I'm no longer in small town Tumbling Shoals, Arkansas. I'm in London, England - what some see as the capital of the world. When I sang that song first I could never have expected what my life would look like. Much joy and fair share of sadness and heartbreak. What I do know is that from the time I first came to faith in Christ, though failing and stumbling along the way, I have sought and will seek to let my light - the light Christ has given me - shine to any and every person

I come into contact with, regardless of generation or background. I pray God will use the honest and very basic challenges of this book to inspire you to do the same.

Your friend

Regan

Glossary of Millennial terms

(AKA - the section containing all the words or expressions that I used in this book that made me feel slightly nauseated and definitely apologetic for my generation.)

Adulting: As stated in chapter 2 this is "to do grown up things and hold responsibilities such as, a 9-5 job, a mortgage/rent, a car payment, or anything else that makes one think of grown ups."

Bantz - Banter

Bare - Very or really. Why not just say 'very' or 'really'. Bare good question.

Basic - This word describes a person or a person's behaviour when he or she lacks originality and just goes along with flow of fashion and trend. That said it also can indicate/mean 'transparent' and 'straightforward'. This is the sense in which I use it.

BFF- Best Friend Forever

Break the Internet - to cause a massive commotion and dominate people's trending viewings and conversations on the world wide web across all social media spheres.

Brohim - Defined by the Urban Dictionary as 'Brother, in the sense of a good friend, battle buddy, fellow traveller of space and time. Often used as a greeting.'

I Can't Even - Speechless, unable to comprehend, unable to deal with, struggling to make any sense in life and of life.

Face-plant - falling face first onto or into something

Fetch - Trendier/fetcher way of saying 'cool'.

Fleek - on point or perfect.

FOMO - Fear Of Missing Out - the opposite of JOMO (not used in this book) which means Joy Of Missing Out

FTW - For The Win...there is a profane version as well, but that was not the one in mind.

GF - Girl-friend

GOAT - Greatest Of All Time

Gone viral - When something is has been shared all over the internet and viewed by thousands as a result.

Humblebrag - a modest or self-deprecating statement on the surface that intends to draw attention to something of which one is proud for a pat on the back.

IDK - I don't know

IMHO - In My Humble/Honest Opinion

Is this real life? - A term used when something crazy just happened. Generally used when one is in complete shock and can't put into words what they are thinking. This can be negative, but it also acts as an exclamation for when something really good has happened and one is extremely happy.

Keep it 100 - Straight talk. Being authentic and true.

Lifehack- Tricks, shortcuts, skills, or unique method to increases productivity and efficiency, in life. Quite often pretty mundane, common sense things souped up for social media.

Lit - something was 'turned up', 'popping', or amazing. Can also refer to being stoned or intoxicated and so is unhelpfully imprecise.

Literally - This one is self explanatory, but it irks me as it is overused and acts as filler word, like - literally - all the time.

LOL - Laughing out loud or Laugh out loud. I know one old age pensioner who signs fairly straightforward and occasionally serious messages with this. It confused me. I now know she believes LOL meant 'Lots Of Love'. Bless her - I don't blame her at all.

NBD - No Big Deal

Netflix and chill - sometimes used to describe simple and straightforward relaxation at home. More often used as a euphemism for illicit hooking up.

OTT - Over The Top

PSL - Pumpkin Spice Latte - I at times have found this slightly tasty although this past year I concluded it was far too sweet and beyond overhyped. Stay away.

Rad - A slangy abbreviation of 'Radical' used as a substitute for 'cool'. Generally an overstatement.

ROFL - Rolled Out on Floor Laughing.

Sorry not sorry - One phrase that you will rarely hear from Millennials is "I'm sorry". Saying "Sorry not sorry" indicates you are perhaps a little sorry that your actions or words have negatively impacted someone, but you're not fully and sincerely sorry.

Squad goals - what you would like you and your friends (squad) to accomplish (goals).

Swear-down - A statement made to signify that what you speak is 100% true. Refers to swearing on or by something or someone else.

TBC - To Be Confirmed.

The struggle is real - generally said when a Millennial is vexed or frustrated by something. This is often used, albeit often unintentionally, in relation to something that really shouldn't cause so much vexatious venting.

Throw shade - To visibly disapprove of something or somebody and to proceed to talk trash.

Turnt up - I used it in the sense of excited and energised. It, however, is often used to describe getting high, or getting loose in action (this can be acting wild in a party sense or by going wild in an animalistic sexual sense).

Woes - Friends, a person's 'squad'

Woke - socially and politically aware

About the Author

Regan Blanton King is a Christian who pastors the Angel Church, in the Angel, Islington, area of London, England. He is a communications officer for life issues with Christian concern. A millennial, Regan lived on both sides of the Atlantic, growing up in Tumbling Shoals, Arkansas. He regularly travels to teach, preach, and train others from the Bible and holds a degree in theological studies from Highland Theological College at the University of Highlands and Islands.